"*And You Will Call It Fate* is a stunningly clear-eyed exploration of masculinity via Timothy J. Hillegonds's long relationship with Sean Dempsey, a man capable of startling generosity as well as unchecked rage. With precision and compassion, Hillegonds maps both the harm caused by Dempsey's fury and the way those same 'toxic' traits helped to propel Hillegonds out of addiction and into a life with ambition and purpose. In short, he sees and holds both Dempsey and himself to account as full human beings. In an era where cultural conversations about masculinity can be dismayingly binary, *And You Will Call It Fate* is exactly the book the world needs."—**KRISTI COULTER**, author of *Exit Interview: The Life and Death of My Ambitious Career*

"Haunting, disturbing, and uplifting, *And You Will Call It Fate* tells the complex tale of a friendship that saved the author from addiction—a friendship as exhilarating and ensnaring as a line of cocaine, full of false promises and flashes of rapture and insight. The character of Sean Dempsey is Hillegonds's Gatsby—enigmatic, lavish in lifestyle, and dangerous to be around. But, like the author of this brave and beautiful book, you'll be glad you came into his orbit."—**MILES HARVEY**, author of *The Island of Lost Maps* and *The King of Confidence*

"Timothy J. Hillegonds has crafted a courageous and unflinching exploration of masculinity, rage, addiction, and redemption. At its core—and perhaps even to the author's own surprise—it's a moving testament to our capacity for transformation and the unstoppable momentum of personal evolution once the will is awakened." —**KATHERINE ROWLAND**, author of *The Pleasure Gap: American Women and the Unfinished Sexual Revolution*

"This is a beautiful thing. A book that tackles the stuff that matters and paints a portrait of life in all of its complexities. The twists of fate. The roads taken and left behind. But mostly choices. The choices we make and the choices we choose not to. It is, in a way, the fundamental question a person must face: taking stock of who we have been and, ultimately, who we choose to be." —**JARED YATES SEXTON**, author of *The Man They Wanted Me to Be: Toxic Masculinity and a Crisis of Our Own Making*

"In his new book, *And You Will Call It Fate*, Timothy J. Hillegonds asks the question: 'To the people who save us, what do we owe?' and his answer is anything but simple. In this extended reflection on failure, redemption, and the limits of gratitude, Hillegonds underscores an important truth about addiction and recovery: that climbing out of the cavernous dark of your own rock bottom is not something you can do on your own. Along the way, though, he asks a single agonizing question: What if the person who helped you out of that hole is wrestling with such demons of their own that they risk dragging you back down? *And You Will Call It Fate* is more than a recovery memoir. It's a story about the grace necessary to see good in people even when they're at their worst, but it's also a story about giving ourselves enough grace to let go of people who stand in the way of true healing. And in the end, it's a story about the humility and courage it takes to stand on your own two feet."—**JOEY FRANKLIN**, author of *Delusions of Grandeur: American Essays*

Praise for Timothy J. Hillegonds's *The Distance Between: A Memoir*

FINALIST FOR A 2020 ERIC HOFFER AWARD

FINALIST FOR THE CHICAGO WRITERS ASSOCIATION BOOK OF THE YEAR AWARD

"The title of this book—*The Distance Between*—captures, not only the miles travelled and the motion created in the story it tells, but as the ending of the book asks us to look forward, the title also conveys something about that space between who we used to be and the people we can become."—**PENNY GUISINGER**, Brevity

"Earnest, well-written, and compelling."—**TIMOTHY PARFITT**, *Newcity Lit*

"If more men were capable of this kind of humility and vulnerability, who knows what changes we might see in our definitions of masculinity?"—**RYAN SMERNOFF**, *Los Angeles Review of Books*

"What a gorgeous book. Hillegonds's candor and insight are a marvel, his storytelling gripping, harrowing, and beautiful."—**MICHELE MORANO**, author of *Grammar Lessons: Translating a Life in Spain*

"With earnest, unflinching prose and piercing detail, Hillegonds chronicles a turbulent past defined by a toxic mixture of rage, recklessness, and addiction. His willingness to peel back the layers of vulnerability and shame to reveal the man he once was is a stirring testament to the man he is now."—**MELANIE BROOKS**, author of *Writing Hard Stories: Celebrated Memoirists Who Shaped Art from Trauma*

"*The Distance Between* is a bracingly honest account of a boy's search for manhood through the wilds of addiction, violence, and early fatherhood. This story gutted me. Hillegonds's debut announces that he's a writer to watch."—**HOPE EDELMAN**, author of *Motherless Daughters: The Legacy of Loss*

"If I could level any criticism against Hillegonds's tour de force memoir, it is that I wish it had gone on for a few more chapters so that we could learn more about his recovery process. Then again, that's not a flaw in the book but a testament to the captivating story it tells."—The (Shepherdstown WV) *Observer*

AND YOU WILL CALL IT FATE

AMERICAN LIVES
Series editor: Tobias Wolff

AND YOU WILL CALL IT FATE

A Memoir

Timothy J. Hillegonds

University of Nebraska Press | LINCOLN

.

The University of Nebraska Press is part of a land-
grant institution with campuses and programs
on the past, present, and future homelands of
the Pawnee, Ponca, Otoe-Missouria, Omaha,
Dakota, Lakota, Kaw, Cheyenne, and Arapaho
Peoples, as well as those of the relocated Ho-
Chunk, Sac and Fox, and Iowa Peoples.

∞

For customers in the EU with safety/
GPSR concerns, contact:
gpsr@mare-nostrum.co.uk
Mare Nostrum Group BV
Mauritskade 21D
1091 GC Amsterdam
The Netherlands

Library of Congress Control Number: 2025039122

Designed and set in Adobe Jensen Pro by K. Andresen.

For Erin, my ride or die

Until you make the unconscious conscious,
it will direct your life
and you will call it fate.

CARL JUNG

Contents

Author's Note

This book is a work of memory, and memory has its own story to tell. I've done my best to convey the truth here, as factually and accurately as possible, but I've concealed the identities of nearly everyone that appears in these pages. This book contains a truth, not the truth.

AND YOU WILL CALL IT FATE

I

ONE

Sean Dempsey was a six-foot-seven Irishman who wore a smirk on his face and a chip on his shoulder from lasting only one week as a defensive lineman for the 1978 Houston Oilers. He and his wife, Summer, came into the Baker's Square restaurant I worked at regularly, usually for a late dinner and a hot beverage, and they seemed to me an unlikely couple. Tall as a bookcase with a blocky jaw and silver hair, Dempsey looked to be pushing a muscular 275 pounds, and his hands were the size of the dinner plates I served his club sandwiches on. Summer, on the other hand, was his opposite: petite, with straight brown hair that hung like graduation tassels just past her shoulders. She drank her Lipton with lemon and honey, and with both hands, too, slowly raising the ceramic mug to her lips in the same way a priest might raise a communion chalice.

Over the course of a year or so, I'd gotten to know Dempsey and Summer in the noncommittal way that most servers got to know their customers. I knew from the short conversations we had as I refilled their drinks and cleared their plates that they had two kids, a boy and a girl, and two muscular pit bulls. I knew they lived in a modernist ranch home they'd built near the edge of a forest preserve not far from the restaurant. I also knew that Dempsey had grown up in Morgan Park, on Chicago's far south side, home to the city's infamous South Side Irish parade.

What I didn't know was what either of them did for a living.

"For work?" Summer responded one night after I asked her, smiling while her tea steeped. "I'm a runner at the Board of Trade."

"A runner?"

"Yeah," she said, pulling her tea bag out of the water and setting it on her napkin. "I work for a broker at the Chicago Board of Trade. I run market orders to the broker's pit trader, wait for confirmation, and then run back to confirm the trade was made."

"Wait," I said. "You mean you actually run? Like a jogger?"

Summer laughed. "Yeah, sometimes. It's fun. Fast paced and a little crazy most of the time. But definitely fun. It's how a lot of traders get their start." She glanced across the table at Dempsey, who was staring at his coffee cup. "You should be a fucking runner, Tim," Dempsey said suddenly, looking up, as if no other discussion was needed. He lifted his coffee cup to his lips.

I laughed. Dempsey used the F-word like table salt.

"Seriously," he continued, putting his coffee cup down. "What are you doing working here? You seem like a smart kid. Do something else. Be a fucking runner." He looked across the table at his wife. "Summer will get you an interview."

"Sure," she said, returning Dempsey's glance. "I'll set it up. The guys over there love me. They'll do it in a heartbeat."

I shifted my weight and fingered the pen in my apron pocket. I knew nothing about trading or the stock market, but I was immediately intoxicated by the idea of being a runner, and it hit me how badly I wanted to do something else, to *be* something else. I truly loved waiting tables—the pace and community and conversations and food, how the work made me feel useful and needed, two things I didn't feel much outside of the restaurant. But every time someone from high school came in and I waited for them to ask me the question I knew was coming—what I was doing with my life or, worse, where I went to college—I fought the urge to crawl under the table. I didn't want to feel that way anymore. I wanted something different. I wanted to give people an answer to that question that didn't cause them to avert their gaze before awkwardly reaching for an appropriate response.

"You don't mind?" I said to Summer. "You'd do that for me?"

Summer smiled and nodded. "Why not?"

Dempsey leaned forward. "Summer will set it up and let you know the details." He paused and looked right at me. "Make sure you show up, Tim." His eyes locked onto mine, and I forced myself not to look away. "Don't make us regret this. Make sure you fucking show up."

I was twenty-four years old when I met Dempsey in 2002, and I had been working at the same Baker's Square restaurant on and off since I was sixteen. By the time we met, I was wearing my hair in true early aughts fashion, gelled and spiked with boy-band frosted tips, and I spent most of my weekends at clubs in downtown Chicago wearing shiny shirts and baggy pants, swallowing ecstasy pills stamped with butterflies or stars or smiley faces or hearts, dancing with neon glow sticks in my hands. I was obsessed with Eminem and electronic dance music, which at the time we called "progressive," and I was a year into a relationship with a young woman named Natalie that was the exact opposite of the last relationship I'd had, one that had played out over the course of three drug-and-alcohol-fueled years more than eleven hundred miles away from Chicago, in the state of Colorado, and had left me with a lengthy criminal record and a beautiful brown-eyed daughter.

Even so, I had enough common sense at the time to "fucking show up," as Dempsey had so plainly put it, so two weeks later, on the morning of the interview, I tucked my brand-new dress shirt into the brand-new slacks I'd picked up at Kohl's and felt an apple-sized knot in my stomach. If I landed the job, it would be the first one I'd ever held that didn't involve stocking shelves or shoveling dirt or wearing an apron. It felt like a shot at a real career, a job I could proudly—and finally—tell my mother and stepfather about without embarrassment.

On the day of the interview, I took a bus from my apartment in Burbank to the Orange Line El Train at Midway Airport and rode the train into the city, staring out the window as it rocked and swayed through the southwest side's largely Polish neighborhoods. I was nervous. I knew how to wait tables. I knew how to drink and party and live an entertaining life earning two hundred dollars a week. What I didn't know was how to conduct myself in an environment where people with college degrees and business acumen would be asking me questions. I was certain they would clock me as the fraud I felt like.

I got off the Orange Line at the LaSalle and Van Buren stop in downtown Chicago, walked across the platform and down the stairs, and merged with a fat stream of people going to work, a shifting amoeba of shiny-shoed bodies that all seemed to have important meetings to get to. I kept pace with the crowd while above me sunlight tumbled from the blue sky, and I was immediately seduced by the alchemy of it all, by the way purpose and opportunity and success hung like humidity in the midmorning air.

When I arrived at the Board of Trade, I checked in with security and took an elevator to the firm's office, where I met with two men in dark suits wearing forced—or maybe exhausted—smiles. I filled out pages of paperwork and fielded questions as best I could, and then they took me on a tour of the building. We walked down a short hallway to a panel of windows that overlooked the trading floor. "This is The Pit," one guy said to me. "This is where everything happens." I surveyed the scene below. The Pit looked like a beehive that had just been kicked. Spread out across the floor were people in all stages of hysteria, yelling, their arms waving above their heads like aircraft marshalers. I asked the man next to me what they were doing. "They're making money, son," he said. "And they're making a lot of it."

Back in the office upstairs, I sat on a chair, nervous, fidgeting with my hands, knowing how close I was to something that felt like it could completely change my life. The man behind the desk picked up my resume with both hands to get a better look then glanced up at me. "So, you didn't go to college?" he asked.

I'd known the question would come, and I'd rehearsed an answer on the train, but it suddenly felt inadequate. "I took a few classes at a community college in the suburbs, but I decided to take a bit of a break. I guess I'm still sort of figuring out what I want to do."

"There's nothing wrong with that," he said. "There's lots of traders that skip college altogether." I perked up, surprised that he was letting me off the hook. "But these guys are still smart. They still passed a bunch of FINRA exams, and they work their asses off every day. It's more street smarts than book smarts down there in The Pit. But it takes commitment and tenacity." He paused, dropped my resume on the desk in front of him, and caught my eyes. "You think you have what it takes?"

I had no idea, but I nodded anyway. "Yes, sir. I do. This is where I want to be and what I want to do."

I rode home that afternoon excited by the idea of being a runner and creating a new version of myself. The train swayed and I leaned my head against the window. Maybe I could actually do something in the business world. Maybe I could entertain a job that didn't send me home with a half-eaten patty melt and hair that smelled like toasted parmesan cheese. Maybe I could be a guy with a closet full of Oxford shirts and wingtip shoes, the type of man who carried a briefcase and read the newspaper.

Two days after the interview, I got a phone call saying that I didn't pass the background check, and just like that, it was over. Not just the opportunity, but the fantasy—the new, professional version of myself I had envisioned. I felt stupid for believing I could ever change who I was in the first place.

The next time Sean Dempsey and Summer came into the restaurant, he knew what had happened, but he asked me about it anyway. I gave him an abbreviated version of my past: the criminal mischief charges and DUI., the assaults, the burglary, the felony for trying to outrun the police, drunk and high, in a borrowed car, and then wrapping it around a pole. Dempsey listened with his head slightly cocked, looking amused. "Well fuck it then," he said and smacked the table with the palm of his hand. "*I'll* give you a job."

I stood there in my condiment-stained bib apron looking at Dempsey, a bouquet of straws sticking out of my front pocket, not sure what to make of what he had said.

"Really?"

"Yep," he said.

"Huh," I said.

And then two weeks later he actually did.

TWO

One night, a few months after I'd returned from Colorado, but before I'd met Dempsey, a coworker dropped me off at my parents' house after working a closing shift at Baker's Square. I was buzzed from drinking at the bar after the restaurant had closed, and instead of going inside and going to bed, I walked down the street to a friend's house. I wanted drugs or vodka or anything that would take me to that place of detachment, that place where everything blurred and I didn't think about abandoning my daughter, or the active Illinois warrant I hadn't dealt with, or the fact that I had been in Colorado for almost three years and come back to the same life I had left.

When I arrived at my friend's house, she was awake, and she knew what I needed. She'd been trying for a while to kick a heroin habit. "All I have is methadone," she said as I stood in her doorway, swaying. "You want some?"

I nodded, because I wanted everything, anything, *all* the things that would make the world shrink and lose its texture—so she poured some of the clear liquid from a small bottle into the cap, and I drank it, and she did it again, and I drank it, and then maybe it was the methadone, or maybe it was all the vodka from earlier, but the world pitched and decelerated and then I was outside again, smoking and walking through the night-soaked air of the neighborhood I had grown up in. The streetlamps spilled margarine-tinted light onto the asphalt and my cigarette left trails like bottle rockets screaming through the summer sky until I was back at my parents' house, climbing the stairs to the front porch. I sat there smoking and thinking, about all the things I was trying not to think about, about my daughter and Colorado and my parents and my friends and my life. It was suddenly so hard to keep my eyes open, so hard to see the world around me, to be in the world around me, and I was fighting the thoughts in my head and the heaviness in my eyes, and then a car slowed to a stop on Central Avenue. I wanted to hide, to be invisible to the car and to the world and to myself, but it was so late and my eyes were so heavy, so I tried to run to the side of the house while a voice yelled for me to stop. But my legs were like stones and there was really nowhere to go, and then the red and blue lights that I thought I'd left behind in Colorado were everywhere, and there were handcuffs on my wrists again, silver and flashing, and I was inside a squad car again—but this time I wasn't in Colorado. This time I was just outside the little house that I loved so much, the one that I had grown up in, and the front door had opened and my stepfather was now standing there, his arms crossed and his lips pressed together tightly, red and blue lights painting the bricks of his house like a canvas.

Although I grew up in the working-class southwestern suburb of Oak Lawn, about twenty minutes from Morgan Park, where Dempsey was from, Chicago was as much a part of me as it was a place, as much DNA as destination, and from the instant I first experienced it as a child, long before I lived within its boundaries, it was with me in every moment.

I grew up experiencing the standard assortment of elementary school field trips that all of Chicagoland's youth were subjected to—the Shedd Aquarium, the Adler Planetarium, the Museum of Science and Industry, the Art Institute, the Field Museum. We'd swarm through massive spaces filled with marble, our voices echoing off the polished stone, our faces pressed to the glass as we pondered Egyptian mummies or brachiopod fossils or enormous bowmouth guitarfish—or we'd sit back in a giant domed theater with our heads tilted upward, where outer space greeted us with a deep and abiding black punctuated by red and yellow planets and stars.

When I was a little older, my mother and stepfather would dutifully pack my brother, sister, and me into their blue Oldsmobile station wagon on the Fourth of July, and we'd drive down 95th Street to Cicero Avenue and turn north toward the Stevenson Expressway, ending up at the Taste of Chicago in Grant Park, which was nestled between a spray of century-old terracotta-faced buildings on Michigan Avenue and the city's titanic freshwater ocean. There, as smoke swirled from grills and around tents and disappeared into blue skies dotted with white clouds and black skyscrapers, and with sweat dripping down the backs of our necks and a crowd of people from every neighborhood in Chicago jockeying for a spot in the shade of the giant oak trees that lined the park, we'd eat Great Godfrey Daniels barbecue turkey legs the size of a man's forearm, and Giordano's deep dish pizza slices so heavy with cheese that no paper plate could handle them, the grease shimmering on our chins and grins plastered to our faces. And then later, stuffed from the food and exhausted from all the walking, as the sun dipped a smidge lower in the west and the air mercifully began to cool, when it seemed we couldn't possibly eat one more bite, we'd laugh as our towering Rainbow Cones dripped ice cream all over our T-shirts.

Later, as a teenager, I was a talented inline skater who managed to turn pro, and I looked to escape the grassy boundaries of Oak Lawn and into the concrete jungle of the city any chance I could get. I'd take a bus, or a train, or catch a ride with a friend and venture into the grid on my skates, grinding all the handrails and curbs I could find, weaving between cars and pedestrians, laughing and flipping off the security guards the building managers had hired to keep skaters like me away. I'd crisscross the city during long summer days of skating with my friends, ignoring all the traffic signals, latching on to the backs of CTA buses as they spewed blue diesel smoke from their exhaust pipes, launching off the Chicago Picasso in Daley Plaza, weaving between the bright red legs of the Calder Flamingo in front of the Federal Building, and then finally, when I was satisfied and happy and utterly exhausted, stopping to take long drags from Marlboro Lights while resting against the back of a wooden park bench as Buckingham Fountain launched water fifteen stories into the sky.

I wasn't sure how it would happen back then, and I can't say that I ever had an actual plan, but ever since that first day I experienced the city of Chicago as a child, when I first peered up at the tracks overhead while crossing Wabash Avenue and heard the bone-rattling knock and screech of the El train, and the percussive honks of the cabs, and the vibration and verve of people moving in and out of alleyways and doorways, going to work or to the bar or to the ball game, I knew that I would make my way there someday, that I would place myself in the middle of the city's wonderful chaos, its beautiful commotion, and I would root myself to the concrete, and become part of the city's fabric.

Dempsey owned a financial services firm located on the thirty-fifth floor of a spaceship-like glass and steel high-rise on the corner of Wacker Drive and Monroe Street, in the heart of Chicago's Loop. I knew nothing about finance, and nothing about working in an office—the closest I'd come was counting the money in the cash drawer behind the closed doors of the manager's office after an evening restaurant shift—but Dempsey didn't seem worried about it. "Come see me on Tuesday," he told me right before leaving Baker's Square one night, not long after my failed Board of Trade interview. "And take the fucking earrings out when you do."

A few days after that, I sat in Dempsey's palatial corner office, which was the size of a small apartment and furnished with an eight-person conference table, two tufted-red-leather wingback chairs, a cherrywood desk and matching credenza, and an enormous throne-like executive chair, on which Dempsey sat smoking a cigar. He exhaled a thick band of smoke. "So what do you think?"

I leaned back in a chair that all but swallowed me, as sunlight sliced in from the wraparound windows, and rays cut like lasers through a haze of cigar smoke. I fought the urge to wave the smoke from my face.

"What's the job title again?" I asked.

Dempsey leaned back in his titanic chair. "Risk Management Coordinator."

I nodded, clueless.

"And what does it pay?"

Dempsey reached across his desk and rolled the ash of his cigar on a large crystal ashtray until a small gray chunk fell off. "Twenty-five grand a year."

I nodded and did the math in my head. It was more than I was making at Baker's Square, almost more than I'd ever made in a year. I turned and looked out the window. Across Monroe Street was another enormous high-rise filled with nice offices and nice furniture and nice people who wore dress slacks and fitted blazers to work. I looked down at my cheap black loafers, my bargain-basement dress pants—I'd shown up for the interview in a slightly cleaner version of my Baker's Square uniform. I didn't have a college degree and I didn't know anything about finance or business, but I felt the same flicker of hope that I'd felt at the Board of Trade interview just weeks before. I could feel how badly I wanted to be part of Dempsey's world, but maybe even more than that, I could feel how badly I no longer wanted to be part of my own.

I met Dempsey's eyes and smiled. Sat up straight while cigar smoke loitered in the air between us. "I'm in," I said as Dempsey leaned back in his chair and stuck the cigar in his mouth. "When do I start?"

The year I met Sean Dempsey, in 2002, I was quickly approaching what I now know was the zenith of my alcoholism. I was still drinking for fun, or at least telling myself I was drinking for fun, and I was still drinking in a way that seemed somewhat acceptable, at least to me. I wasn't hiding it from anyone, like I'd been doing after things had spiraled in Colorado, or pawning my possessions for vodka or drugs, and I felt that qualified me as normal. But I knew on some level—even deep in that denial—that I was actually a meteor burning up in the atmosphere of my life, a thrown rock headed for a window.

One of the first few days I worked for Dempsey, while I sat in my cubicle surfing the internet, he came up behind me and kicked the wheels of my rolling chair with his wingtips. "The fuck are you doing, Hillegonds?" I jumped and spun around. Dempsey was grinning. "I, uh . . ." He cut me off. "I'm just fucking with you, Tim. Get your shit. We're going to lunch."

I did as I was told, and a few minutes later we walked across Wacker Drive to the historic Civic Opera Building. We took an old-fashioned elevator to a members-only restaurant on the top floor called the Tower Club, and a maître d' greeted us in a black tuxedo. "So good to see you again, Mr. Dempsey," he said, smiling, bowing forward ever so slightly. "Please, follow me."

The maître d' took us to a small, round table that was draped with a white tablecloth and set with polished silverware and gleaming water glasses. Around us, the room was lush—dark wood on the walls, thick curtains drawn to keep out most of the noontime sun, Tennessee marble and gold leaf accents. As a waiter filled my water glass and I eyed the basket of artisan breads he had placed in the center of the table, I became aware that I had never been to a restaurant as nice as this one before. I felt like an outsider and an impostor, but, inexplicably, I also felt like I belonged there somehow, like the working-class family and life I'd had in Oak Lawn had all been leading to this place, this palatial art deco building that was designed by the architect to look like a throne, where I found myself believing for the first time in my life that it was possible to become something other than what I already was, or what I thought I should be. I looked across the table at Dempsey, who was smoothing his napkin onto his lap, his shoulders nearly spanning the width of the table, and for a moment I wondered why he was doing this, why he had hired me, a young man he didn't know, without any reasonable work experience, and given him a chance. Not long before, after breaking up with my daughter's mother and completely spiraling in Colorado, I had been homeless and sleeping in a back booth of the Denny's I worked at. Now, just a few years later, I was drinking filtered water out of spotless crystal glasses. It was nearly impossible to comprehend.

"What are you going to have?" Dempsey asked, snapping me back to reality. I narrowed my eyes. *All of it*, I thought, before smiling and ordering a sandwich.

Finance, I soon learned, had a language all its own. *Equity, portfolio, dividend, asset, liability, yield, leverage, arbitrage, derivative*—they were the words that I learned how to pronounce first, before actually understanding what they meant. When I used them in sentences those first few months, they felt foreign to me, not unlike the Spanish I had tried and failed to learn in high school. I sat in meetings with a notepad and a pen, clueless, writing down words, hoping they'd somehow take root. "It'll all start to make sense at some point," Dempsey's business partner, George, said to me as we left a meeting one afternoon. "Hang in there, son."

To complicate things even more, if someone had asked me about my title, about what a Risk Management Coordinator was, and what one did, I couldn't yet describe it. All I knew for certain was it had something to do with the handling of financial claims. In meetings, Dempsey often talked about "fighting for the individual," and "not settling in court like those fucking empty suits at traditional finance companies," and he'd often talk about it with such intensity, and with so much profanity, that I sometimes wondered if he meant actual fighting, like with fists, or crowbars. That wasn't what he meant, but I knew he wouldn't be opposed to the opportunity if it ever presented itself. I'd noticed that on some days, Dempsey would walk into the office with such gruffness, such bearishness, that the briefcase hanging by his side resembled a medieval flail, a weapon he might use to clear out an elevator full of people with one hard swing.

George had told me that I could stop by his office anytime I had questions, and it became clear to me that he was the finance expert behind Dempsey's operation. While Dempsey could read a room and change its temperature with his presence, which had its own strategic advantages, he didn't have the financial pedigree that George had. Dempsey was a former football player used to knocking grown men horizontal. George quietly tended to spreadsheets. Dempsey preferred to kick down doors to the rooms he wanted to do deals in. George simply knocked and then presented a thoughtful, calculated plan.

The thirty-fifth-floor office was fairly small, with only a handful of other people who worked there, and during the first few months of my employment, I got to know some of my coworkers through small talk over coffee in the lunchroom. Janet, the office manager, was a southside Irish Catholic mother of two boys with a great Chicago accent and a pocketful of entertaining stories about working with Dempsey over the years. Gerald, a cocksure underwriter who smelled of Winston cigarettes and Brut cologne, took an early train from the suburbs and arrived first at the office every morning. There were two women named Melissa and Melanie who handled administrative tasks I didn't understand, another underwriter named Peter who sat quietly in his office most of the day and never answered his constantly ringing phone, and a young woman about my age who was nearing the end of law school. We'd pass each other in the long hallway on our way to and from the restroom, giving each other a quick glance and a forced smile, and I couldn't help but think about how different we were, how when I was serving breakfast-for-dinner to senior citizens at Baker's Square and swapping my maple-syrup-sticky dollar bills for twenties, she was taking "Advanced Topics in Property Theory" at John Marshall Law School.

In so many ways, in Dempsey's office, I felt like a charlatan. I didn't know how to format a spreadsheet or make coffee in the commercial coffeemaker, and I was still learning how to comport myself in a professional business setting, but Dempsey liked me and it seemed as if maybe that was enough. "Just fucking pay attention, Tim," he'd say to me after meetings. "And write everything down." To my credit, I would. I didn't always know exactly what I was writing, but the simple act of taking what I heard and putting it down on paper, which wasn't all that different from taking orders at a restaurant, helped me remember terms and phrases that would have otherwise remained elusive. For the first time in my life, in a large conference room where I sat scribbling notes on a legal pad, I had a seat at a table where I wasn't serving the meal.

Sometime during the first year I worked for Dempsey, I took a day off to appear in court on an old misdemeanor charge—driving on a suspended license, drug paraphernalia—I hadn't yet dealt with since returning from Colorado. I walked into the District 5 courthouse in Bridgeview and made my way to the docket to see what courtroom I was supposed to appear in. As I stood there scanning the piece of paper hanging on the wall, there was an unmistakable voice behind me. "What are you doing, motherfucker?" I turned and saw Dempsey standing there, a grin plastered across his square jaw. "You gotta be kidding me," I said, feeling my face run pale as I calculated the odds of running into my boss at the same courthouse, on the same day, at the same time that I had to be in court. I stared at him with wide eyes. "What are *you* doing here?"

Dempsey nodded to a man standing next to him, a lawyer by the look of his matching oxblood shoes and briefcase. "Same thing you are, I guess. Gotta pay the piper."

I eventually got the story from Dempsey—he'd "gently nudged" a woman with his shopping cart at the supermarket near his house. "What can I say?" he said from behind his mammoth cherrywood desk a few days later. "The old bag wouldn't move so I persuaded her with the edge of my shopping cart." He took an enormous drag from the Padron he was smoking in his office, despite repeated warnings that it was against the fire code. He blew the smoke out slowly and smiled. "Who knew it was a fucking crime?"

Dempsey's rage was the stuff of legends, and the stories were abundant. He'd once thrown a stapler across his office when the manager told him the electric bill was months overdue and the lights were about to be shut off. He'd once, in college, fought five guys at the same time, dropping each of them with thunderous right hands. He'd once, in a drunken rage at the bar in the office building's lobby, lifted the jukebox off the ground and thrown it across the room.

By the time I'd hit my one-year anniversary with Dempsey's company, I'd witnessed his rage on a number of occasions, and it was sometimes funny and sometimes terrifying. I was riding shotgun in his car once when he tried—and nearly succeeded—to run an SUV off the Eisenhower Expressway because the driver, a man who seemed oblivious, had cut him off. Dempsey's jaw had clenched like he was biting down on a mouthguard while he weaved in and out of traffic, swerving onto the shoulder, rocks pinging off the undercarriage, until he got right next to the guy, not caring that the vehicles' exterior door handles were nearly touching as he reached across me to get his middle finger as close to the other driver's face as possible.

In the office, when Dempsey was on a conference call, he often had it on speakerphone, and his profanity-laced tirades spilled outside his open door and down the hallway. "Really?" I'd hear him yell. "You don't *think* that's a good idea. I don't give a rat's ass *what* you think, motherfucker! That's what we're doing!" Minutes later I'd hear his heavy footsteps storm past my cubicle, the paper clips on my desk vibrating in their plastic tray.

The longer I worked there, the more stories I heard: Dempsey made a Starbucks barista cry for screwing up his order. Dempsey was escorted off a United flight for arguing with the flight crew. Dempsey pulled a teenage boy through a Burger King drive-through window after he'd found out the kid had broken up with his daughter.

In the moments that I saw Dempsey give in to his rage, it scared the shit out of me, but I also envied it. Dempsey's anger and dominance shaped a type of poisonous, aggressive masculinity that—at that point in my life—I fundamentally craved, if for no other reason than that I had spent so much time on the receiving end of it. In the years just after being expelled from high school, I was a skinny teenage skater with long hair and baggy pants, a stoner, a rebellious kid willing to break the law and drink and drug his way to an alternate reality, but I wasn't tough, at least not in a physical sense. I was emotional and afraid during confrontations, often too scared to throw a punch, and it was the part of me that I despised the most. I'd had my ass beaten in street fights a number of times because I couldn't back up the shit I was talking, and even though I understood that Dempsey's behavior was wrong on every level, that his version of masculinity was indeed toxic, I also understood that he was protected and insulated from the world in a way that I was not, but desperately wanted to be.

"I don't know why I do it," Dempsey once told me after he'd lost his temper, in a way that made me think he truly didn't understand. "I'm really trying to work on this anger thing."

What's that like? I remember thinking. *Having that much rage inside just waiting to come out?*

But then I thought about it some more and realized I knew. When it came down to it, I was just like Dempsey. Our rage simply manifested in different ways.

His came out as abuse against the world.

Mine, as abuse against myself.

Sean Dempsey commanded attention in every room he entered. In conference rooms, people turned their heads and stopped their conversations. At restaurants, people glanced up from their plates when he passed by. This was partly because of his NFL football player stature—he was almost always the tallest man in the room—but it was also because he was handsome and knew how to dress. His face was naturally tanned, and he wore stylish dark-framed glasses, his graying hair always neatly parted. His slacks were pressed and his shirts and suitcoats were custom-made by a haberdasher who stopped by the office every couple of months with a smile on his face and fabric samples in his briefcase.

To say that I was captivated with Sean Dempsey doesn't quite get to the heart of what I felt once I began working for him. I was completely enamored with him. I was fascinated by the way he brought his cigar to life with the blaze of a wooden match, his face glowing orange as he drew and released his cheeks, smoke billowing out like storm clouds in a Midwestern sky. I was fascinated by the way he drove his black Mercedes with the seat pushed all the way back to accommodate his long legs, his right hand draped over the steering wheel, the interior smelling like leather and tobacco. I was also fascinated by the way people reacted to him, their voices suddenly unsure of what they were saying if the expression on his face changed when they were speaking. He was like a symphony conductor holding a baton, the rest of us violin players with our hands gripping our bows, waiting for the signal to play.

Two

In meetings, I studied him. I watched as people leaned in close to hear him, listening intently to every word he was saying, in part because they were interested, but also because he spoke so softly he was sometimes difficult to hear, which I came to understand was strategic—there's no better way to get someone to listen than to make them strain to hear. I scribbled notes on my legal pad and jotted down words I didn't understand, and slowly I began to learn—about business, and about this business world that neither I nor anyone in my immediate family had ever taken part in. When I watched Dempsey from across the conference room table, often wondering what the hell I was doing there in the first place, it was as if I were looking at the version of myself I'd always wanted to be: a successful man who took no shit, and had taken an unconventional road to get there.

One night during that first year that I worked for Dempsey, at a seafood restaurant on Navy Pier overlooking Lake Michigan, I asked my girlfriend, Natalie, to marry me. The moonlight flickered off the water as I slid out from the booth with a nervous smile, dropped to one knee, and presented her with the platinum and diamond ring I had asked a friend to cosign on because my credit was so bad I couldn't get a loan by myself. She smiled her big smile and said yes, even though I'm sure she must have wondered how I had paid for it, and the restaurant broke out in applause.

I like to think that we meant the words we said to each other that night. I like to think that we truly intended to spend our lives together. That we were going to get married and take our two different worlds—the one in which her father, whom she adored, was a judge, and the one in which my father, whom I despised, was a concrete contractor—and we were going to bring those two worlds together to create a new one. She would finish her degree and probably go to grad school. I would work my way up in Dempsey's company and make lots of money. We'd live a nice life in a nice house somewhere in the suburbs, and everything, to be sure, would be easy.

But nothing about my life was particularly easy, especially not for Natalie, who was sometimes tasked with being more of a babysitter to me than a fiancé. It was true that I'd gotten the job with Dempsey and a career seemed suddenly possible, but I still drank and used drugs the way that I always had: recklessly and without remorse, and without any sort of understanding of how my behavior affected everyone else.

At the time of our engagement, I lived in a small suburban apartment a few miles from Midway Airport. To get to work, I had to take a bus to the Orange Line El stop at Midway and board the train headed for the city. But on most days, I'd be too hungover to hear my alarm. I'd awake too late to make it to the bus stop, and I'd lean over and wake Natalie, who often stayed over, and beg her to drive me. "Come on, Nat," I'd say, my voice still gravelly from last night's cigarettes, my eyes slits that felt glued together. "You know I can't lose this job, right? I need this job. *We* need this job."

No matter how inconvenient it was for her to drive me, or how late it made her, or how shitty I made her feel with my unwarranted guilt trips, she would always do it. But my late nights and hungover mornings, combined with the fact that on more than one occasion I'd spent my entire paycheck on alcohol or cocaine before the weekend was over, had taken their toll on our relationship, and it was starting to show. "There's no off switch when you drink, Tim," she said more than once on our drive to the train, as I looked out the window while we passed gas stations and hotels that rented rooms by the hour on Cicero Avenue, wincing from my hangover. "Normal people don't get hammered on a fucking Tuesday night. They just don't."

When Natalie finally broke up with me, it was the matter-of-fact nature of it that stung the most. There was no drama. No huge fight. No overturned tables or broken dishes. The day it happened, I was driving her car to a friend's house when she called. "I can't do this anymore," she said. "Do what?" I said into my cell phone, not understanding, annoyed. "This. You. Us," she said, before abruptly hanging up.

There was a resolve in her voice that felt authentic, and I knew she meant what she said, but I told myself it was temporary and acted like I didn't care. I parked her car at my friend Ronnie's house like she asked me to, keys hanging from the ignition, door unlocked, and when I looked out the window a little while later, my chest just beginning to warm up from the vodka I'd begun drinking the instant I walked in the door, the car was gone—and so was she.

Shortly after we broke up, when it was clear that we were truly done, I moved downtown with my best friend, Richie—he had paid the down payment and bought all the furniture, including an enormous big-screen TV—and into a beautiful condo, on the sixteenth floor of a midrise, with polished hardwood floors and a balcony that overlooked a park. It was a new place and a new start, and I acted as if the breakup didn't bother me, like I wasn't devastated by the fact that I had asked a woman to marry me and then refused to make any steps toward being a responsible, or at least not irresponsible, person. But instead of learning from my mistakes and trying to right my wrongs, instead of changing direction, I burrowed deeper into all the things that numbed me—drinking and drugs, bars and clubs, the slowed-down fog of my haphazardly manufactured life.

I tried to keep it from Dempsey, the fact that holding my life together was getting harder and harder, but it was impossible to hide. I was tired all the time, mostly because I was hardly sleeping, instead spending my nights at bars with Richie or alone with my bedroom door closed, snorting cocaine and watching porn until my alarm clock went off, desperately trying to feel something other than failure. During those cocaine-fueled nights, I thought often of my daughter, who was growing up without me, of the relationship with her that I'd all but given up on. I thought often of Natalie, too, whom I missed more than I would admit to anyone, and I simply didn't want to feel everything I was feeling—hate and anger and failure and disappointment—so I snorted cocaine until my nose was so packed with mucus I could hardly breathe and drank until I could no longer control my bladder.

I'd show up at work in clothes that weren't pressed, with bloodshot eyes and greasy hair, and try to play it off, disappearing into the bathroom to splash cold water on my face, chewing peppermint gum nonstop. It was impossible to hide, though, especially from someone like Dempsey, who I'd learned was an alcoholic in recovery himself. He'd often leave the office just before noon, telling the receptionist he was going to a "meeting," which I later understood to mean A A *meeting.* He'd brought sobriety up only once with me, when we were sitting in the bar of the Biltmore Hotel in Miami, him smoking a cigar, me drinking my third vodka-Seven. "That shit almost did me in," he said, nodding at my drink. "Turned me into a fire-breathing dragon." I laughed self-consciously, stirring the ice with my straw.

Now, on a cold winter morning more than a year into my employ with Dempsey, after I'd taken off my jacket and draped it on the back of my chair, hungover yet again, he pulled me into his office. "You're fired," he said, in a way that seemed more resigned than angry. I looked down at the floor and my eyes teared up. I was unable to muster an excuse for myself. I simply sat there in that space between what he had said and what I had yet to say, knowing I had a negative balance in my checking account and was fifteen days late on my rent. "Okay," I finally managed. "I'm really sorry, Sean."

Later, after I'd grabbed my coat and taken the elevator downstairs, after I began crying on the Monroe Street sidewalk, my shoulders shaking in my jacket, Dempsey called my company-issued cell phone. "Look," he said, while a bike messenger whizzed past. "If you're willing to admit that your life is unmanageable, then I think I can help you. I learned a long time ago there's an easier, softer way. Your life doesn't have to be this hard."

I didn't believe what Dempsey was saying, but I listened and nodded anyway, and then I said "okay" as cars drove past, not knowing at all what he was talking about, not knowing rehab was what he meant.

II

THREE

On January 28, 2005, at roughly two o'clock in the morning, just one week after Dempsey had fired me, I bent over the bathroom vanity in the downtown Chicago apartment I shared with Richie and inhaled a line of cocaine. I watched through the mirror as a granule fell from my nostril and bounced across the polished marble. I was tired and scared of what awaited me.

Six hours later, with bloodshot eyes and a claw in my stomach, I boarded a plane and flew to a drug and alcohol rehabilitation facility about an hour outside of Minneapolis, Minnesota. I was twenty-six years old.

In the seven days that had passed between Dempsey firing me, then calling me back and saying he'd find me a bed in the same rehab he'd attended years before, and then indeed finding me that bed, I'd spent every dollar I had to my name—five or six hundred dollars that I'd hidden in various places in my bedroom—on alcohol and cocaine. I wanted to forget about all that had happened, not just with Dempsey and the job I had lost, which I knew I had been all-too-fortunate to have in the first place, but also about all that had happened before that—the breakup with Natalie, the legal mess I'd left in Colorado, the fact that I'd left my daughter without a father.

Richie was out of town for the week, which meant I was left to my own devices, which meant that I could drink and use without reservation. So that first night after I'd left Dempsey's office, before he'd even called to say that he was sending me to rehab, I'd begun drinking. It was cheap red wine at first, from a bottle that had somehow sat unopened on top of the fridge since Richie had left, and the wine did what it always did, spackling the cracks inside me, filling in the holes, covering up—at least for a while—my state of disrepair.

When the wine was gone, I called my coke dealer, and not long after he answered, not long after I had traded nearly all the money I had to my name for the white, powdery contents of a crinkled plastic bag, I was back in my apartment alone, snorting line after line of cocaine, making the lines longer and thicker, chopping and scraping them with the hard edge of an expired Chicago Public Library card, my heart thrashing as if it might thunder right out of my rib cage and onto the floor.

For years I would look back on that moment, at that time I spent alone and sitting on the edge of the couch in the living room of my apartment in the darkness of the early morning, hundreds of dollars behind on rent, my checking account overdrawn, my cash all but gone, determined to inhale every bit of cocaine I had purchased, and wonder if that was the moment a change had begun. In the moment it didn't feel like I was changing, and nothing about my behavior suggested that I was, but it felt as if I had finally collided with a force, an energy, that had my full and undivided attention. I was going to rehab and that meant something. Rather, it defined something. If I was going to rehab, then it meant that I was a person who needed to go to rehab, and I could no longer deny what I had become. I wasn't yet willing to use the words *addict* or *alcoholic*—it would take time to locate those words and accept them—but something inside me was shifting, something inside me had moved.

In Minneapolis, woolly snow blew across the tarmac as I deplaned. I was tired and cranky and no longer high. As I emerged from the jet bridge, a man who seemed about a decade younger than my grandfather approached me. He had kind eyes and wore a wheat-colored

Carhartt jacket unzipped, a black-and-white checked flannel shirt tucked into his jeans. "Tim?" he asked. I nodded, swallowing my nausea. "Great," he said, smiling. "We've got one more person to pick up, and then I'll drive you guys to the facility."

I'd spoken to someone from the rehab the day before, and they'd told me that a transportation liaison would be meeting me at my gate. I'd had to provide them with a description of what I would be wearing, and it dawned on me in that moment that preselecting my outfit for the following day was the most planning I'd done in years. Everything before that moment had simply been a reaction.

I grabbed my suitcase and walked with the old man toward a gate on the other side of the airport. I was tired from staying up too late the night before, tired from the flight, already—not even a half day in—tired of trying to get sober.

I yawned as we weaved through the crowd, passing a Hudson News and a coffee kiosk, the smell of beans somehow comforting, wishing we could stop. I thought about asking if we could, but the man leading the way was moving pretty quickly and I decided against it. I glanced over my shoulder just as a man ran past dragging a Rollaboard behind him, his suit coat billowing in his wake.

A few minutes later, the old man I was following arrived at the gate he was looking for, stopped near a garbage can, and swiveled his head until he spotted a young man sitting on a chair by the wall. He had a small suitcase he was using as a footrest and a large guitar case on the floor beside him. He had long brown hair and a swollen black eye that looked relatively fresh. "I think that's him," the old man said. I had no idea whether it was him or not, so I just nodded and followed as he walked toward the man with the black eye. He grinned as we approached.

"You guys the rehab crew?" he asked.

The old man nodded. "Yep. Grab your stuff and we'll make a break for it."

The guy with the black eye, who looked to be about my age, shifted his feet off the suitcase, stood up, and grabbed his guitar case.

"You can bring that thing to rehab?" I asked. He shrugged. "Guess I'll find out."

I turned toward the window and watched as a plane taxied out to the runway, its lights flashing.

Above me, the PA system crackled.

Outside, the plane's engines roared.

According to the old man who had picked us up, the drive from Minneapolis–St. Paul International Airport to the rehabilitation facility in Center City would take about an hour. I climbed into the van first and sat next to the window. The man with the black eye followed, slid into the seat next to me. "Here goes nothing," he said.

I half laughed then said, "You got that right."

I hunkered down in my seat and was suddenly struck by the realization that I knew almost nothing about rehab except for what I'd seen on television and what Dempsey had told me on our last phone call before I left. "It's going to be good," he'd said. "They'll put you back together." I'd nodded into the phone as if he could see me, and like I agreed, but I knew nothing about rehab could possibly be good. And how could they put me back together in there? Dempsey had no idea just how far I'd come apart.

In the months leading up to the van ride, my drinking and using had seemed to reach a sort of crescendo. There were days when Richie and I would talk over lunch, him in the suburbs working, me in the city at Dempsey's office, and I'd say to him, "Tonight I'm going to get so fucked up I can't remember my name," and he'd say, "Hell yeah, I'm right there with you," and that's what we would do. Those nights would always end with lines of cocaine, of which there was never enough, and when it was finally all gone, all the alcohol and drugs, after night had turned into morning, and then late morning, and then afternoon, I'd be left to myself in my room, lying on my unmade bed, trying to sleep but unable to, the depression I felt like a wet blanket lying across my face, making it hard to breathe. I would despise myself in those moments, replaying the night before, wishing I could somehow undo it all. I knew it was unsustainable in the long run, that I couldn't party the way that I did, but I didn't know how to not do it, how to not be the person I so clearly was.

Up front, the old man pulled a worn Minnesota Twins baseball cap low over his eyes and put the van into gear. "Settle in, boys," he said, turning the wheel as we pulled away from the parking garage. "Let me know if you want me to change the radio station." He adjusted the volume and I recognized an old song by Creedence Clearwater Revival that reminded me of my stepfather. I thought back to the last conversation I'd had with him and my mother a few days before I'd left, when I'd told them I was going to rehab. I called them right before I went to meet my dealer, after the wine had given me the courage I needed to make the call but before the cocaine made me paranoid. I felt like such a failure when my mother picked up, like such a colossal fuck-up. I was reminded of all the other times I had called them in moments like that, moments where my life had spiraled, like in Colorado when I called collect from jail, asking to be bailed out, listening to them say no, or when I was homeless and on the run from the police, warrants issued and ready to be served, nowhere to turn, begging them to Western Union me some money. Now, after I told them where I was going and why, they said I was doing the right thing, and that they were praying for me, but I wondered what they really thought of me. Did they really think I was capable of change? Did I?

As we drove, the old man occasionally glanced in the rearview mirror, and I saw that his eyes were sunflowered by creases. He looked content and benevolent, and I wondered if he'd been doing this for a while—shuttling broken people to and from rehab. I wondered if maybe he'd once been like us.

Outside, snow had been pushed to the edges of I-35, where it piled up, gray and dirty. The van vibrated down the highway, and I stared out the window trying to imagine what rehab was going to be like. I wondered what they would say to me when I got there, what they would make me do. This was just temporary, right? Just a quick break in the action so I could get my shit together? It had to be. There was no way I could make a decision to change forever. I wasn't even sure what that meant. Permanent just sounded so . . . permanent. I just needed a little help. A little help to figure out how I could drink and use like a normal person.

The passing world blurred into a long gray and white brushstroke. From my seat, I could see the passenger side mirror, and I watched as a miniature Minneapolis faded even further into the distance behind us, getting even smaller, soon replaced entirely by the dark greens and browns of the forest, branches drooping and heavy with snow.

"I'm not supposed to do this," the old man suddenly said from up front, as if he could somehow sense the uncertainty we were both feeling. "But do you guys want me to stop for cigarettes?"

"Yes," we said in unison, sharing a relieved glance, grateful for this one last thing we could count on, this thing from our previous lives, this one last kindness before we walked through the doors to change.

The rehabilitation facility seemed more like an Ivy League college campus than the rehab I had imagined in the week leading up to my arrival. It was nestled up to a lake on a beautiful piece of property that had once been a working farm, surrounded by forest and field. There were separate dorms for men and women and strict rules to not talk to anyone of the opposite sex, as well as a large dining hall, an auditorium with maybe a couple hundred seats, where we would gather for each evening's speaker, a meditation center, a medical unit, and a recreation center complete with an Olympic-sized swimming pool.

Not long after arriving and handing over my luggage to be searched and cataloged, and then undergoing a physical exam, I sat in a small office across from a man wearing olive chinos, dark brown loafers, and the type of button-down shirt that could also be used to work in the garage. It was late afternoon by now, and the light was fading. Behind me was a small window that looked out onto a long patch of land covered in snow. In the bottom corner, ice spiderwebbed outward.

"I've read your intake notes and the results of your physical exam," he said, shifting in his chair and crossing his right leg over his left. "All things considered, you're in pretty good physical health. But I'm still going to ask you a few follow-up questions. Sound good?"

I caught his eye for a moment, nodded, and looked away. The last place I wanted to be was right here, in this room, talking about my train wreck of an existence.

"It says here that you're currently experiencing problems in your life due to your alcohol and cocaine use. Is that right?"

I looked at the floor. Felt a flash of frustration at the sheer absurdity of the question. "Well, I sure as shit didn't come to Minnesota for a vacation," I said.

He smiled, as if he'd heard that one before, and then looked down at the papers covering the legal pad in his hand. "So, for eight years you've been drinking just about every day. Says here that vodka's on the menu pretty regularly, last use yesterday at 4:00 a.m. Beers amount to about twenty or thirty at a time, sometimes spread out, sometimes over the course of a day or night. Last use was yesterday as well. Also says here that you use about seventy-five dollars' worth of cocaine three or four times a week, and your last use was early this morning, at 2:00 a.m." He paused and looked up. "How's my math?"

I thought back to the paperwork I'd had to do when I arrived, all the ways they had asked me to quantify my partying. *How many days a week do you drink? How many drinks do you have? How much money do you spend on drinking? How often do you buy drugs? In what quantity? At what price?* It felt like an economics exam. His math didn't seem exactly right. But it didn't seem all that wrong, either.

"I don't know," I said, "it's sort of impossible for me to say. All I know is I drink, I mean I *drank*, a ton and did a bunch of coke and somewhere along the way everything fucking unraveled." I thought back to the night before, to the cocaine I'd bought from my dealer, to the line I'd done in the bathroom of my apartment, to how tired I'd looked when I'd stared at my face in the mirror. "I don't know," I said. "I really don't. But what the fuck. Does it really matter? I'm here regardless, right?"

The counselor leaned back and uncrossed his legs, then re-crossed them on the other side, then rested his hands on top of the note-pad in his lap. "Yes and no. It matters from a medical standpoint, Tim. We need to know if you're suffering from withdrawal." He seemed to be waiting for a response from me, but I didn't give him one. Instead, I found a spot on the carpeting between us, where I imagined a small flame bursting from the Berber, engulfing the office in fire. He continued, nonplussed by my lack of eye contact: "It doesn't matter in the sense that that was then and this is now. And now is what matters."

I looked up at him, feeling somehow softened. "Yeah, but now is what I'm worried about." I thought about Dempsey back at the office waiting for me, about Richie, who'd probably just found out that I was going to be gone for a while at rehab, about my daughter, whom I'd been thinking about nonstop since I'd arrived. Without drugs or alcohol, without anything to quiet the noise inside my head, it felt nearly impossible to be inside my body.

"Just hang in there, Tim," he said. "You know what they say: one day at a time."

I shook my head and looked back at the floor. A day at a time still seemed like far too much to handle.

A few days into my stay, I received a package from Dempsey containing a small leather-bound journal. It looked expensive, and I imagined Dempsey picking it out at one of the locally owned parchment stores on Dearborn Street, near the cigar shop where he sometimes bought his Padron cigars. I'd gone there with him a few times, feeling so grown up, so professional, so important as I stood next to him while he talked with the owner, or sitting across from him on a black leather chesterfield sofa, the smoke like a curtain between us. Now I sat on the edge of the twin-sized bed in the room I shared with a meth addict named Keith and turned to the first page, where I found a note written in his elegant cursive letters. "Dear Tim," it read. "I'm very proud of you for taking this important step. You can do this! Please have an open mind to what you will see and hear there—it was the best decision I ever made, and I am confident you will gain immeasurably. Remember, life is good and will get better for you when you come home."

I closed the journal and stared at the cover, suddenly feeling the weight of what Dempsey was doing for me, something I'd not really thought about since I'd arrived. At first rehab had felt more like a punishment than a gift. I'd been so focused on myself, on pitying myself, that I hadn't even taken the time to acknowledge Dempsey's remarkable generosity, that not only had he paid over twenty-thousand dollars for me to attend this rehab, which I'd recently learned was lovingly referred to as the "Rolls Royce of rehabs," but Dempsey had also decided to keep paying me while I was there, which meant I could still pay my child support, which meant I wouldn't fall further into arrears. He'd also told me that there was a possibility I could come back to work for him after I got out. "We'll see how it goes," he'd said. "But for now, just focus on the shit that's in front of you."

At that moment, what was directly in front of me was a writing desk with a small chair pushed in underneath it. Next to me was another twin-sized bed with a writing desk and chair in front of it. Down the hall were more chairs and more desks and people having conversations. I turned the journal over in my lap and ran my finger across the stitching.

Life is good and will get better for you when you come home.

I closed my eyes and my throat tightened. How could he know if my life would get better? How could he possibly fucking know? Behind my eyes, I felt the wet of my tears. I didn't want to open them, to let loose the water, to feel what I was feeling, which was completely unworthy of all of it—the job downtown, the bed at rehab, the chance to make a change. Why would someone do all this for me? I didn't deserve it. I could never repay it. It was as if not having the answer made it even more impossible to bear.

I soon learned that the man with the black eye I had ridden in the van with was named Jason, but all the men in my unit called him Jesus because his hair was long and his name started with a "J." His eye was starting to heal, and greens and blues and purples bled out into the area around his eye. I asked him about it. He told me he had a fight outside a bar and had to take a few to give a few. He said maybe he took too many and didn't give enough. I laughed and told him I understood.

Early one morning, Jesus walked by the bathroom, where I was vigorously scrubbing the toilet because I'd been assigned bathroom duty for the week. We had a rotating chore schedule, bathroom cleaning being the worst of them, and they had to be completed each day before our morning meditation, which wasn't really meditation in the traditional sense, but a quiet time where we, still half asleep, reflected on a passage from an AA book called *Reflections*.

"Dear Jesus," I said when he was right outside the door. "Dear Jesus, can you perform miracles?"

"Of course," he said, stopping and leaning against the doorframe. "My dad's a bigwig. You might say I've got family in high places." He paused for effect, didn't even try to hide his dumb grin when he spoke again. "But they frown on the water into wine thing in here."

I rolled my eyes.

He said, "What'd you have in mind?"

I bent over the toilet and swirled the bristle brush around the bowl. It created tiny blue bubbles that smelled like mint candy when they popped. As I swirled, I thought about all the miracles I needed—forgiveness from my family, money to see my daughter and pay the back child support I owed, abstinence. Each miracle seemed more impossible than the one before.

I stopped swirling and looked up. "I'm not sure yet," I said, "but I'll let you know." I paused for just a second. "Fair warning, though, Jesus, it's going to be big. I'm going to need a big miracle."

Jesus smiled. "You know where to find me," he said, flashing an index finger skyward, then pressing his palms together in front of him in the praying position. He bowed. I shook my head and laughed. He turned to walk away and then stopped and looked back. His long hair swayed and framed his face on both sides, like theater curtains. "Have faith, my son," he said. "Have faith."

A week into my stay, I again sat down in the chair across from my counselor, and it was faith that was on his mind. It was midmorning. Through the window behind me, sunlight flooded into the room. Through the window behind him, sunlight bounced off the snow-covered field. The sky was a resplendent cornflower blue.

"Let's talk about where you're at spiritually," he said.

"Spiritually?"

"Yeah, spiritually. Got any thoughts on the subject?"

The question caught me off guard. There hadn't been a whole lot of spirituality in my life during the years that led up to this stint in rehab, none to be found in the bars I frequented, or at the dealer's apartment, with its overflowing ashtray and always-on television. I tried to deflect. "My parents are Christians," I said. "So, you know, that's how I grew up."

"Okay, but that's not what I asked. Christianity's a religion. I asked about spirituality. And I asked about you, not your parents. So, let's try this again. Where are you at with spirituality these days?"

I'd been in rehab long enough to hear some of the quotes that I would later learn defined AA, and one had stood out to me. *Religion is for those who fear hell, spirituality is for those who have been there.* I wasn't exactly sure what it meant, but it resonated.

"I guess I don't really have a good answer right now," I said, shifting in my seat, glancing out the window behind him. The sun was as bright as it had ever been, shining down on the snow, beautiful in its brilliance. "I'm still trying to unpack all of this."

I'd been sober for a week, the longest string of days I'd put together in years. I could barely wrap my mind around that fact in itself, let alone conjure up a coherent thought about spirituality.

My counselor reached over and picked up a coffee cup he'd set on the side table next to him. He took a sip then pondered the cup for a minute before putting it back on the table. "I get that you're still trying to figure this all out, that you're just starting to put together a vision of what your sober life might look like. But I want you to think about this idea—that spirituality can be something separate from religion. I'm not trying to tell you what you should or should not believe, but I am trying to get you to decouple these two ideas."

I thought about what he was saying. I'd never before considered that spirituality and religion could be separate, that I could choose to put down one and still hold the other. It felt blasphemous to even think that—the guilt was strong and immediate, and my heartbeat shifted up a gear—but it was also, simultaneously, freeing to contemplate. The story I'd been told my entire life was that I was a broken sinner who needed to repent, that I was unworthy, that the only way I could be saved from eternal damnation was to say a prayer and give my life over to the Jesus of the Bible, the one born of a virgin, the one who was supposed to be just like me but seemed nothing like me, the one who took on the sins of the world so I could be free for all eternity. A broken sinner, damaged, unworthy—was that the story I had internalized? Was that why drinking until I was completely numb felt so good? Because I felt like I was living into my true identity, doing all the things a broken, damaged, unworthy sinner should do?

I shrugged. "I don't know. I think I get what you're saying, but it's a lot to process."

"Indeed, it is," he said, "but it's worth the effort. I can promise you that. There's an insight to be had there."

"How do you know?"

"Sit in my chair long enough and you see a few things, come to a few conclusions."

I leaned forward and propped my elbows on my knees, folded my hands and rested my chin on them. Religion and spirituality, salvation, they weren't concepts I had spent a whole lot of time thinking about since childhood Sunday School. But just then I could feel a thought take root. Maybe this whole experience, meaning everything that had happened—getting the job from Dempsey, then losing it, then shipping off to rehab—maybe it was actually *all* about salvation. But maybe it wasn't a salvation I could find in the Bible, or through any of the characters in it, or even a salvation that was tied to a religion. Maybe it was a different kind of salvation altogether, one delivered to me not by a carpenter from Nazareth, but by a big and sometimes angry man named Dempsey, the man who'd given me this chance, this incredible opportunity to see the lighthouse of recovery through the fog of substances.

Days later, with the temperature flatlined somewhere in the teens, I stood with a mouthy New Yorker named John on the concrete patio just outside our housing unit smoking cigarettes and shivering. We'd hit it off in the first group session and had begun spending a lot of time together. We were around the same age, midtwenties, and shared a love of pizza that was borderline obsessive. Above us, the sun burned cold and yellow in the sky, and the snow that quilted the field and lake and the entire treatment center campus was on fire with brilliance. It was strange, I thought, how beautiful and serene this place was. How there could be peace and beauty in the midst of all this turbulence.

John kicked at a piece of ice that had frozen to the concrete. "I'm supposed to tell my story tomorrow night," he said, his Staten Island accent thick and sloppy. "I fucking hate that part."

I walked to the edge of the patio and took a step into an area of untouched snow. Made a footprint with my sneaker while taking a drag from my cigarette. "What do you mean 'tell your story?'"

John looked up at me. "You don't know this? It's textbook rehab shit, man. They put you in a chair in the front of the room, and everyone else stares at you while you talk about how you got to be all fucked up."

John seemed to be waiting for a reaction from me, so I nodded. I thought back to how it was that I got to be all fucked up. The trouble I'd been in when I was younger, a DUI, misdemeanor assault, felony eluding, drug possession—a lot of it involved substances. I'd never really thought substances were the problem, though. They had seemed more like a solution. A release. Or just the way twentysomethings passed the time on weekends.

I glanced over at John. "You know what you're going to say?"

He looked at the ground, started kicking at the ice again. "I'll probably just say what I've said every other time I've been to rehab."

"Which is what?"

"The story of all the fucked-up things I've done and how I just want someone to fix me."

"I feel you on that," I said, taking one last drag and walking over to the ashtray. I stubbed out my cigarette. "If you find that someone," I said, turning toward the sliding glass door that led into the unit, "be sure to let me know."

My roommate, Keith, was older than me, though I couldn't tell by how much. Some days he seemed like he was a decade older. Other days, more. Tall and lean with messy dark hair and wild eyes, Keith had a bone-crushing handshake that, when I grimaced, he said came from a lifetime of turning wrenches.

"Why are you here?" I asked him one day after a group meeting, as we were walking down a narrow hallway back to our room.

"Meth," he said. I thought back to the meth I'd done when I lived in Colorado, the way it made life speed up and slow down at the same time. I'd smoked it and snorted it for a few months, at one point knitting together five days with no sleep, but, somehow, I'd managed to get away from it, to somehow leave it in my past. I sometimes thought about how I was lucky to leave it behind, to not end up a meth addict like Keith. But the reality was that I was just lazy. Alcohol and cocaine and ecstasy were so much easier to get once I got back to Chicago. And anyway, it dawned on me, we'd ended up in the same place regardless.

"Do you think this shit's going to work?" I asked.

"What shit?"

"This shit," I said, nodding my head toward the big room where we all sat in the circle for our group meetings, where blue Big Books were lying on the chairs, where all of us would at some point tell our stories. "Rehab."

Keith looked toward the great room, then back at me. We rounded the corner and walked into our room. "I don't know, man," Keith said, sitting down on the end of his bed. "It has to for me." He paused, and I leaned against the doorframe to watch him. "My life is a fucking train wreck, man."

I nodded and thought about my own train wreck, about Dempsey waiting for me to get out, about the daughter I didn't see. I'd have to fix things with her, somehow, if that was even possible. It all seemed like too much of a mess to clean up.

Keith got up from the bed and walked over to the window and looked out onto the snow-covered field. He turned around to face me. "This shit has to work, man. It literally has to. Because I don't know what the fuck else there is."

In the next session with my counselor, he sat across from me with a small stack of papers on his lap. "Why don't you read problem number three on your worksheet out loud a minute?" he said. "I want to spend some time on this."

I was two weeks into my stay—the halfway point—and I'd fallen into the routines of rehab. I awoke, made my bed, completed my chores, attended meditation and morning group, ate breakfast, wrote in my journal, managed to find the inside of the gym, read the Big Book, smoked cigarettes, and met with my counselor almost every day. I talked to Jesus and Keith and John about how our lives were going to be different once we left. We all had so much hope, so much dewy optimism. *Things will be better*, we said. *We'll make it*, we said. It felt like our lives before, like my life before, the life of only two weeks ago, the life of drinking and using, was an alternate reality we'd once visited, or a movie we'd once watched but only sort of remembered.

I scanned the stapled pages I held in my hand until I found what he was talking about on the worksheet. "Problem number three says that cross-addiction, self-will, and immaturity are roadblocks to step one for me."

"And what's step one?"

"That we are powerless over alcohol and our lives have become unmanageable."

He shifted in his seat. "Do you believe that?"

I hadn't believed it when I'd arrived, but I was starting to believe it now. At least part of it. Between the group sessions and the reading I'd been doing, I'd begun to realize that the way I drank and used wasn't normal. Normal drinkers didn't regularly piss and sometimes shit themselves in bed. Regular drinkers didn't hide twenty-dollar bills from themselves so they wouldn't spend every penny they had on partying and not be able to eat the day after payday. Regular drinkers didn't snort lines of cocaine so they could sober up just enough to drink some more. And yet, I wasn't sure I was completely sold on the idea of abstinence, of never drinking again. I still held on to a distant thought where maybe I could just figure out how to drink and use normally. Was it really too late?

I leaned back in my seat. "I believe that my life is unmanageable. But it's hard to see how I'm powerless over a fucking liquid. I mean, it doesn't make any sense. Alcohol can't actually *do* anything."

My counselor smiled. "But you're here, right? So it may not have actually done anything, but it certainly contributed to some things. Would you agree with that?"

"Sure, but that doesn't mean I'm powerless over it."

"Did you ever wake up in the morning with a hangover and tell yourself you were going to stop drinking?"

"Yeah," I said, annoyed. "So?"

"And what happened?"

"You know what happened."

He set the papers on his lap, grabbed the arms of his chair, and hoisted himself up so he was sitting straighter and looking right into my eyes. "Look, I'll cut to the chase here, Tim. The idea isn't that you don't have agency over your life, because you absolutely do. A lot of what you're learning in here is about accountability, right? About taking responsibility for your circumstances? The idea isn't that you don't have control over your actions. The idea is that if you get in a power struggle with alcohol, alcohol is going to win—every single time. So how do *you* win?"

The question hung there between us. I didn't have an answer, so I just looked at him, not sure of where this was going.

He continued, his energy growing. "You win by not getting into the power struggle in the first place. You win by not picking up. You're powerless over alcohol, but only when you invite alcohol in and give it the power. You're not powerless to avoid it. Long-term sobriety is about strategy, Tim. It's about figuring out what's going to help you continue down this path to sobriety, and what's going to get in your way—or worse, move you in a different direction." He paused and took a deep breath then picked up the papers on his lap and pointed them toward me. "You read earlier about cross-addiction, self-will, and immaturity being blocks to step one, right? You know what that's evidenced by?" He brought the papers in front of him and tapped a finger right in the middle of the page. "It says right here: 'Patient self-reports living a lifestyle based on alcohol and drug addiction, self-will, and self-centeredness resulting in negative and painful consequences.'" He paused again and looked right at me. "Step one is about admitting powerlessness, sure. It's about humility and getting rid of your monster ego. But it's also about *reclaiming* power. You reclaim the power of your life by admitting powerlessness over alcoholism and chemical dependency."

I leaned forward and put my elbows on my knees. What he was saying made sense to me, but sobriety still seemed like so much work, and so hard to imagine. I'd never known a sober version of myself. Who would I even be?

I shook my head and looked down at the floor. "But what if I can't do this? What if I get out of here and it's right back to the same shit?"

"You can do this, Tim."

I sat back up. "But what if I can't? What if I *actually* can't?"

His face relaxed and I could feel the energy in the room shift and soften. "Listen to me, Tim. You can. You can do this. It's new and hard and scary—I get it. But you can do it. Don't overthink it.

What do you always hear guys say in here? Don't drink, and go to meetings. That's it. That's the blueprint."

I leaned forward again and rubbed my face with my hands, then I clenched my eyes shut. It couldn't possibly be that simple, could it? I opened my eyes and my counselor was looking at me, taking me in. I looked back, uncertain, scared.

He smiled. "You got this."

"Maybe," I said.

"You do," he said, standing.

I took his cue and stood. I felt unsteady on my feet.

"Look," he said. "Whatever you think your life is going to be like when you leave here, Tim, it's going to be different from you imagine. Better in some ways. Worse in others."

"Is that supposed to be helpful?"

"I'm just being real with you. But for now, just keep it in perspective." He nodded toward the door. "Same time tomorrow, Tim. Keep your head up."

"Yep," I said, turning toward the door, thinking about the blueprint, thinking maybe it would be better if I just never left rehab at all.

On one of the coldest nights of my stay in rehab, John told his story, and a few nights later I did too, sitting in a chair positioned at the front of the room, the entire group of men I lived with fanned out on mismatched chairs in a half circle in front of me. I was terrified and uncertain of what I was going to say, but also somehow energized, and not long after I'd begun talking in a voice quiet from fear, something inside me broke free, a dam that had been holding everything back, and my voice steadied and picked up pace. There was so much that had happened in the years after I'd been expelled from one high school and dropped out of another, in the years that I'd lived in Colorado, so much that I'd been trying hard to forget. There was so much that I hadn't told anyone about, not Dempsey or my parents or even Richie—but in front of those men, in a place that felt safe, I unloaded all of it, telling the whole and unfettered truth of the matter, the reality of the person I'd been in those mountains: the one who'd been arrested more times than he could remember, who'd spent two months in jail, who'd once approached a defenseless man in the street, robbed him, and used the money to buy shiitake mushrooms from the grocery store and tried to sell them to some guys at a park. The one who'd eventually fucked with the wrong people, people who wanted to hurt him, or worse; the one who'd been so scared that he bought a gun for protection and filed off the serial number because that's what they did in the movies, the one who'd had that pistol tucked in his waistband in a grocery store parking lot when the men who'd been after him approached, the one who'd fingered the grip on the gun and had been ready to pull it free but somehow, inexplicably, miraculously, stopped.

In front of those men in rehab, as I told my story, as I told the worst and most shameful parts of my story, perhaps for the first time since I'd returned from Colorado, from the mountains where so much had changed for me, I saw and felt just how differently my life could have turned out, and how serious it all was, and just how close I was to making a decision I couldn't come back from. I could finally feel the weight of what it meant for me to escape that place, and to escape myself, and to have met Dempsey, and for him to give me the opportunity first for a job, and then for rehab, and ultimately, as I would eventually unearth, years removed from that moment, for a life.

As I sat in front of those men, unloading all of it, confessing my sins, I suddenly understood what my counselor had been trying to tell me about the difference between spirituality and religion. I suddenly understood what he meant, what the saying I'd heard was trying to convey: *Religion is for those who fear hell, spirituality is for those who have been there.* In front of that group, in front of those men, so many of them just like me, with stories just like mine, I felt a divine connection, a spiritual bond that transcended religion, that affixed us to one another. Our stories were our confessions, yes, our accounting, our inventory, but they were also our prayers, our pleas, our invocation to each other and to the universe that everything we'd once been could be transformed, and remade, and renewed into something else. Our stories were our petitions, our appeals—and in that room in a place far from home, in a place that just weeks before I'd never even heard of, I felt that I'd been baptized and made free, awash in a newfound gratitude for life.

More than an hour after I'd begun, I was exhausted from the purge, and each of the men in my unit came up to me, individually, and hugged me. *You're in the right place,* they said. *It's not too late,* they said. *You can change,* they said.

When it was John's turn, he stopped just in front of me. "Good shit, man," he said. "You got this. Don't fuck around. Stay sober. Be a dad."

I wanted to speak, to respond, to tell him that I would, but my voice was caught in my throat. Instead, I nodded. He took a step forward and hugged me.

In his embrace, my tears came fast and hard.

When someone was leaving rehab—we called it graduating—we all gathered in the great room for a goodbye ceremony the evening before. All sixteen of us sat in a circle on those banged-up metal folding chairs, fidgeting and caffeinated, the air scented by just-smoked cigarettes, feeling some emotion that was hard to pin down, some mix of worry and jealousy and excitement and gloom. Like everything in rehab, the ceremony was confusing. Someone was graduating and we were happy. Someone was graduating and we were sad.

During each graduation, we passed two objects around the room: the graduate's now-worn AA Big Book, which we'd all been issued after intake, and a bronze thirty-day coin imploring: *To thine own self be true.* When the book arrived, we wrote notes to the graduate and signed our names with the date scribbled beside them, knowing that that day, that moment, somehow mattered more than all the others. When the coin arrived, we placed it in the palm of one of our hands, pressed both hands together with the coin in the middle, and closed our eyes in a prayer of sorts, transferring to the flesh-warm metal whatever goodness we had located inside ourselves during the days we'd spent sober.

When John was graduating, I wrote a note on the inside cover of his book. "You're an amazing dude, John, and I know this time is different. I've heard the way you've been talking in here and you *get* it this time. You really do. If you ever need anything, I'm here. Just take it one day at a time."

After we had all signed John's book, the counselor invited him to stand in the middle of the circle. He handed him his thirty-day coin. "We're all proud of you, John," he said, and John studied the coin in his hand, pondering one side and then the other, slowly rubbing it between his fingers and his thumb, then squeezing it into his fist. Thirty days between his old life and his new one. Thirty days between what used to be and now. John looked at the counselor and then he looked at all of us. His eyes were wet and grateful.

No matter who was graduating, it was a moment we all loved to watch. As John stood before us, searching for words in a moment that seemed too big for them, I watched him from my seat, imagining what the coin felt like in his hand—warm, weighty, substantial. In a few days it would be my turn to stand in front of the group, just twenty-four hours removed from returning to the life I had left behind, to Dempsey and the world that awaited me, thirty days now separating my old life and my new one, what used to be and now.

In a few days it would be my turn to stand in front of the group, watching my Big Book make its way around the room, saying my goodbyes, giving out hugs, fingering the warm and weighty coin in my pocket.

And then before I was ready, before I felt even remotely ready, I was once again in a van with Jesus and the old man who had delivered me to rehab, his hat once again pulled low over his eyes, the music punctuating the ride, headed to the airport, terrified of reentering a life that now felt like a foreign country. I was thirty days sober and wanted to stay that way, but as the airport got closer, the reality of what that meant began to settle in. I was changed in every way that mattered on the inside, but on the outside, I looked the same, and the life I was going back to, the one I'd left just one month before, was exactly the way I'd left it.

As we arrived at the airport, the old man pulled the van to the curb. He put the van in park and turned to me in the back. "Ready?" I stared at him, lost for words, not ready in the least. "Ready as I'll ever be," I said.

The old man smiled at me and opened the door. A few minutes later I was pulling my suitcase behind me, glancing up at the flight schedule, thinking about work, hoping I wouldn't let Dempsey down.

III

FOUR

We call it rehabilitation, meaning to restore someone to health, but it might be more accurately defined as "interruption," meaning an extended break in an addict or alcoholic's behavior. The hope is that the interruption lasts long enough for some of what the patient does in rehab, known simply as "the work"—talking with other addicts and alcoholics, reading about the ways addictions can manifest in one's life, reflecting on past actions, weeping, going to bed early, getting up early, doing chores, eating regular meals, exercising—fuels a realization within the addict or alcoholic that their old way of doing things—what AA calls being left to one's own devices—isn't healthy or productive or helpful.

In my case, and for reasons I still don't entirely understand, the interruption worked. I spent four weeks in that snow-covered facility an hour outside of Minneapolis, with no phone and no contact with the outside world, save for a few phone calls to my mother and stepfather, and one fateful phone call to my daughter's mother, in which I told her that I was going to change, to really change this time, and that I would be in my daughter's life from that point forward—and something inside me shifted. I didn't yet know what that shift was and what it would ultimately mean, and I had no idea how difficult sobriety would become, how hard it would be to face myself and the people I'd hurt, and how tedious and frustrating it would be to make small changes in my life. But in the space provided by that prolonged interruption, where I was forced to slow down and feel, to simply be with myself no matter how uncomfortable it was, I was remade.

After twenty-eight days, I was thrust back into the outside world, against the advice of my counselors, who wanted me to either stay longer or transfer to a halfway house. At the very least, they suggested, I should find a place to live that didn't expose me to friends who were still drinking and using. Their suggestions were well intended, but they were also impossible. I was deeply in debt and I couldn't afford to live anywhere else. The best I could do was ask Richie not to keep alcohol in the apartment.

Much to my relief, Dempsey wanted me back at work as soon as I was discharged. "We'll see how it goes," he said on my first day back, as I sat in the same wingback chair I had been sitting in when he fired me just a month before, and when he had hired me a year before that. "If it works out, it works out, but you don't owe me anything." He took a long draw of his cigar and blew the smoke out into the air above him. "I did this for you, Tim, but I also did it for me. When it comes to sobriety, you have to give it away to keep it."

When Dempsey had left rehab a handful of years before, he'd gone right back to work and thrown himself into it with the same intensity he brought to his new, sober life. He expected me to do the same. "Show up early and stay late," he said to me one day as we stood in the hallway next to a wall of towering filing cabinets. "Show me that you fucking give a shit, okay?" I nodded and said okay, because I absolutely did give a shit, but I was also unsure of exactly how to do that.

I threw myself into work after rehab with the same sort of intensity I imagined Dempsey had manifested some years before. I had a myriad of accounts to settle, with both my loved ones and myself. I had literal accounts to settle, too, in the form of unpaid medical bills and credit card debt, child support I was late on, utility bills that were overdue, and money I owed Richie. In the first months of being back in Dempsey's office I calculated every financial debt

I owed and wrote the totals on a sticky note I hung on the wall of my cubicle. Each time I got paid, I allocated ten or twenty dollars, whatever I could afford, to each of the accounts, and then I crossed out the old total and wrote the new one. They were nearly imperceptible adjustments to the amounts, but they were a type of progress I could see and be proud of, a type of visible progress I never remembered having had before.

For my first month home from Minnesota, I balked hard at the idea of attending ninety AA meetings in ninety days, as they had suggested I do in rehab. AA seemed repetitive and boring and cultish, and I felt smarter and better than the people I saw in those rooms. So I didn't attend meetings and instead convinced myself I could live a life similar to the one I'd lived before rehab, only without the alcohol and other substances. And then one night perhaps a month after I'd returned home from rehab, on a night that dripped with nostalgia for my old life, when I felt that familiar desire to be outside myself, to not feel myself, to disappear into the comforting oblivion of substances, I went with Richie to a bar. It was a weeknight and I should have been in bed, and I think I knew that, at least on some level, but it felt so good to rebel, to nurture that destructive part of myself, to know the right thing and do the wrong thing anyway. I wanted to be out, to be part of the city's ether, to feel the Epsom-soak of the nighttime air, to feel the skin-prick of desire from not knowing where the night would lead. I stood in a bar with Richie in the early hours of the morning, sober, as the lights flashed and the music played, trying to have fun, trying to lose myself in the music the way I used to, staring at the shimmering bottles on the shelf. All around me people were drinking and laughing and dancing, and for a moment I felt something that I can only describe as danger. I suddenly wondered why I was there and what I was doing, and just as I began to think that maybe, just maybe, this bar on this night wasn't where I wanted to be, Richie came up to me.

"What's up?" he said.

"Do you want to get some pills?" I said, not knowing where the words were coming from, as if someone else were saying them.

Richie looked at me, puzzled. "You sure you want to do that?"

"Why not?" I said. "It's not like I was addicted to ecstasy."

And then before I knew it I was dialing my dealer's number, and the line was ringing, and the music was playing, and the people were dancing, and Richie was looking at me in a way that seemed both concerned and excited. My heart was pounding and then a voice was talking on the other end of the phone, and it was my dealer's voice, and I was about to ask about the pills, about a whole handful of pills, and suddenly I realized it was my dealer's voicemail, and it felt in that moment like my heart might explode. I looked around once more at the people, and the lights, and the look on Richie's face, and I knew I couldn't be in that place, that bar, for one more second, because I knew for certain in that moment something I hadn't known until right then—I wanted to be sober. I didn't want to drink and I didn't want to take pills and I didn't want to lose the small amount of sober time I'd amassed, because it suddenly mattered in a way I could physically feel. In the frame of time that existed between the flash of light and the pulse of music, I felt everything I'd worked through in rehab, all the tears I'd cried and all the conversations I'd had with men who were just like me, all the promises I'd made to stay sober, to work The Program, to not do what I was doing in that exact moment. I felt the weight of all the late nights I'd lain on a hard mattress on a twin-sized bed in Minnesota, staring at an unfamiliar ceiling, vowing to myself over and over that I was going to be a different person, a responsible one, a better one. In that small stitch of time, I was given a sort of grace—and I understood. I snapped the phone shut and put it in my pocket, and I told Richie *I have to go, I have to go right fucking now*. He nodded his head and said okay, and we moved toward the door. I felt the air on my face and the night glistened on my skin, and the city lights danced from the buildings and my heart beat loudly in my chest and my breath quickened and then, finally, we were in the back of a cab and headed to our apartment. I knew in that moment that I had been saved from myself, by a power greater than myself, by a force I couldn't name but felt, and I was grateful I'd made it out of that bar, and that I'd somehow held onto the thing that mattered most: sobriety, the gift I'd been given, which I had just discovered I wanted.

Back at the office, I felt unmoored. I wasn't sure how much my coworkers knew about my situation, but they knew something, and I tried to hide the discomfort I felt over them knowing my story with a hastily manufactured level of bravado and confidence. In some ways, I felt like the golden child—and like I was untouchable. Dempsey had sent me to the Rolls Royce of rehabs, paid for my stay, and even continued to pay my salary while I was there—and I felt special because of it. I should have been filled with gratitude and humility—things we'd talked about daily in rehab—but I was still the same cocky, immature person I was before I'd left, only now I was sober. I didn't know it of course—or maybe I did, but didn't care. But Dempsey saw it. He saw it in the way that I held my chin up when I walked through the office, and in the way that I chewed a toothpick in meetings, and in the tone I sometimes used when I answered a question. And one day he pulled me into a meeting with a few other people in his office—guests who were visiting from London, important business associates of Dempsey's who had the power to make decisions that could change the trajectory of the company. And maybe I was tired that day, or just thinking about something else in my life, maybe about sobriety or money, or about Natalie, who'd recently found out that I'd been in rehab and was upset that I'd chosen to finally get sober long after the chance to put our relationship back together had passed. But partway through the meeting, as I sat quietly, half-listening, doodling on the pad of paper that I'd brought to take notes, Dempsey suddenly slammed the table with his fist so hard that my pen bounced off the stationery. I looked up at him, wild-eyed, knowing I had fucked up but not knowing exactly how, and his eyes narrowed and his face reddened. "What the fuck!" he roared. "What the fuck is wrong with you?! Who the fuck do you think you are, you selfish, ungrateful piece of shit? Not paying attention and doodling in your notebook like a fucking schoolboy? How dare you?!"

I didn't dare. I didn't dare move, or say anything at all, and I could feel my face flush as my heart pounded and the pen trembled in my hand. Dempsey was as mad as I'd ever seen him. The other people in the meeting were staring at Dempsey, their eyes wide and their lips glued together, and they had begun, unconsciously it seemed, to push their chairs back from the table. Dempsey half stood, as if he were going to crawl clear across the tabletop to grab me by the neck, and I instinctively leaned back even though we were six feet apart. He leaned forward with both hands, palms down. The vein in his neck plumped, thick and ropey, and he clenched his jaw and spoke through his teeth. "I'll tell you one thing, you smug piece of shit. You better find some *motherfucking* humility and you better find it right the fuck now."

The tears arrived without warning, and I did all I could to hold them back. I knew I couldn't cry in front of those people from London, or in front of Dempsey. I couldn't show him how weak I was. How uncertain. How lost. I couldn't confirm for him what he already knew—that all the confidence and cockiness that I had walked around with every day since I got back from rehab was really just an act, and I was terrified.

I dropped my pen. I still hadn't said anything—what was there to say?—and I got up, avoiding Dempsey's eyes, and walked out of the meeting, feeling a hotness burn through me as I passed him, and down the hallway to the bathroom. Once inside, I tried to calm myself, to suppress the emotion inside of me, but I was embarrassed and hurt and, worse, I was exposed.

I cried hard and fast, and I hated myself for every tear. My shoulders shook and my eyes emptied. When it was over, I splashed water on my face and rinsed out my mouth. I spit in the sink. I stared at my reflection—at the red of my face and the red of my eyes, at a new sober self that felt completely undone. I fucking hated Dempsey in that moment. I fucking hated him for how weak he'd made me feel. How powerless. More than that, though, I hated him because I knew that everything he'd said to me was true. I *was* cocky. I *was* ungrateful. I *was* smug and selfish and absolutely terrified of my new life, of the sober version of myself that I was still getting to know. But I also understood what needed to happen next, what I needed to do.

I gathered myself as best I could and opened the bathroom door. I walked down the hallway and back into Dempsey's office. He glanced at me as I passed him and took my seat. He didn't stop talking or acknowledge me in any other way. I picked up my pen and flipped my notepad to a clean page, free from doodles, and began taking notes again. I looked up and met Dempsey's eyes, and I held his gaze for a moment. Some unsaid thing passed between us—perhaps a recognition of sorts—and the meeting continued as if nothing had ever happened.

As I sat there in my discomfort, my eyes red from crying, wanting, quite literally, to be anyplace other than where I was, I suddenly understood the fundamental truth of the moment: This was what humility felt like.

In the weeks and months that came next, I committed myself wholeheartedly to the same two things that Dempsey did: sobriety and work. I found an almost divine sense of purpose in both. I attended

AA meetings at the Chicago Mercantile Exchange on Wacker Drive and inside the brown-brick walls of the Monadnock building, the largest office building in the world when it was completed in 1893, and at the beautiful Gothic Fourth Presbyterian Church, the second oldest building on Michigan Avenue north of the Chicago River. I listened to stories of women and men who had done unspeakable things and then changed their lives, and I began to see that I, too, could change. I wasn't sure what or whom, exactly, I was changing into, but I followed the blueprint that I'd learned in rehab and I began to carve out a life that had a predictable structure to it. I went to work. I went to the gym. I went to meetings.

At the office, my hard work was rewarded. Dempsey saw the changes that I'd made in my life. Just like he had instructed that first day back, I was often the first person to the office in the morning and one of the last to leave, often in my gym clothes—and he was proud of me. On some evenings, when Dempsey was about to leave for the day, he'd stop by my cubicle to tell me he was headed out. I'd walk with him to the elevator and then down to the lobby, and then down to the parking garage and over to his black Mercedes, which was almost always washed and shining under the bright white industrial lights. "What are you doing this weekend?" he'd say. "Nothing much," I'd reply. "I'll probably hit the gym and then a meeting." Dempsey would smile and nod and then reach into the pocket of his slacks. "Here," he'd say with a smile, pressing a hundred-dollar bill into my palm. "Get yourself a nice dinner tonight. Live a little."

In those moments with Dempsey, I felt something I can only describe as love. I wasn't his son and he wasn't my father, but we'd bonded in a way that blurred the lines of our employer-employee relationship. He'd thrown me out of meetings and screamed at me until I felt my upper lip trembling, and he'd once balled up a report I'd printed out and handed him and thrown it back at me like a snowball, but underneath all that anger and frustration was love. I knew that he cared about me. I knew that he wanted to see me succeed. He wanted to toughen me up, I think now, to show me that the world wasn't going to celebrate my sobriety and that I needed to be prepared to claw and fight for it. More than that, though, I think he wanted me to understand that when it came to living a sober life, the stakes were as high as they could possibly be. He understood in a way that I did not that all of it—the sober days I'd amassed, the little bit of money I'd started using to pay down my debt, the civil communication I'd begun to have with my daughter's mother—could be gone in one night, with one drink or one line, with one misplaced priority. Long before I ever did, he understood the fragility of it all, and how fleeting it all could be.

I was determined to make good on the promise I'd made to my daughter's mother in rehab—that I'd be in my daughter's life from that day forward—and my ex and I had begun communicating fairly regularly since I'd been back in the real world. She was skeptical of my sobriety, and my commitment to it for that matter, but she was open to having me come for a visit with our daughter. By that time, in 2005, I'd been gone from their lives for five years.

But the logistics of flying to Colorado to see my daughter were complicated. I had an active warrant in the state that stemmed from an unresolved court matter that I'd simply skipped out on years before, and I was so deeply in debt that after paying child support and my creditors, and giving Richie my half of the rent, I sometimes didn't have enough money to buy more than a day or two's worth of groceries. Buying a plane ticket felt completely out of reach.

In AA meetings, I often heard old timers say, "Just do the next right thing," and I had begun trying to live my life according to that philosophy as much as I could, but I was often confused as to what the next right thing was. I paid what I could to the bill collectors who called my office phone regularly each week. I went to meetings. I showed up at the gym even on days when I didn't feel like it. I did my best to stay open to what the next right thing was, and then I tried to do it.

I'd begun working out in rehab as a way to break up the monotony of recovery. I was just going through the motions in the beginning, but something had clicked once I started moving my body again, and ever since I'd returned from rehab, I'd kept at it. The physicality of the gym, of working out muscles that hadn't seen real exercise in years, of getting my blood flowing and my heart rate up, had given me a way back into my body, into the athlete self that had defined so much of my youth and young adulthood—the athlete self that I had abandoned once I started drinking and using.

I worked out at a Bally's Total Fitness near the office, located in the basement of a high-rise building on the corner of Adams and Franklin. I was a regular there, showing up rain or shine after work to kill time and get a sweat going, and in the days since I'd been coming, I'd gotten to know a trainer named Andrea, an energetic brunette from Rhode Island with an accent she'd held on to even though she'd lived in Chicago for more than a decade. She trained clients while I struggled to run a full mile on the treadmill, and between sets and clients, as I caught my breath and she readied her next workout routine, we talked. I learned she had a deep and abiding love for animals, especially dogs, which she fostered throughout the year—mostly pit bulls, which often bore scars from being forced to fight or from living on the streets. She was quick with a smile, and gracious with her compliments, and before long I found myself telling her parts of my story, about Dempsey and rehab and my new sober life. Eventually, I told her about my daughter.

"I just have to fix things with her," I said to her one day, as I leaned against the metal doorframe of her office. "I know it's going to take time and work, but none of this shit matters if I can't fix what I broke. I need to be in her life. She needs to be in mine."

Andrea looked up at me from her worn and weathered office chair. "I know," she said, her voice filled with genuine compassion.

"You'll figure it out. You just need to take the first step and go see her. She's seven now, right?" I nodded, thinking about how much she'd grown in the time I'd been gone. "So, she's still young, but she'll understand when you tell her how you feel about her. She'll forgive you, Tim. She will."

I didn't know if Andrea was right, but I knew I needed to get back to Colorado to find out. I was scared, though, terrified of everything I'd left behind. The thought of going back there, to where my life had spiraled so completely out of control, to where I'd gone to jail and fallen into a life of bad decisions and questionable choices that had nearly killed me, even though I'd finally see my daughter again, had me nearly paralyzed with fear.

In those early days of sobriety, everything felt unbelievably complicated. I was six months sober and just starting to make sense of my new substance-free life, but the novelty had worn off. I was lonely and depressed, suddenly thrust into an existence that I couldn't share with anyone I knew in any meaningful way. Richie was still going out and partying with the same group of friends, and I missed them all dearly, but I knew that if I was going to be sober, if I was going to *stay* sober, I needed to do something different with my time. But "something different" often meant "something alone." I was trying to figure out where I fit into my life—or if that was even a possibility, if there was still a life I fit into. I went to work and to the gym and to meetings, and I walked around the city in the evenings, watching the windows of skyscrapers blaze to life around me as the sky began to darken, staring out at the vast blue expanse of Lake Michigan, where red lights blinked on top of the UFO-like water cribs that pumped water into the city, doing my best to be grateful for the chance I'd been given—but I now felt the enormity of it all, the magnitude of what putting my life back together really meant. Even though I was allocating as much money as I could to the bills I owed—child support, back child support, medical and dental bills I hadn't paid for years, a gym membership that had gone into collections, a computer I'd financed but abandoned payments on—the progress was excruciatingly slow. No matter how hard I worked, or how diligently I tried to budget, it seemed like the totals I'd written on the paper taped to my cubicle wall almost never went down and I was almost always broke, to the point that one morning, as I tried to board the El to work a few days before payday, I ran completely out of money and couldn't afford the train fare. I stood near the entrance to the station by the newspaper machines, frustrated, dejected, and finally summoned the humility to begin asking people who walked by if they could spare a dollar or two. I tried to explain as best I could, but I knew how ridiculous I sounded, and looked. I was wearing a dress shirt and dress slacks, and I must have sounded like I was lying, and hardly anyone met my eyes, and no one dug into their pocket, and, in that moment, I realized that this was what sobriety would be at times. I could do the next right thing over and over, I could pay the bills and go to meetings and fold the laundry, but it sometimes still wouldn't be enough to shield me from the natural consequences of my actions, regardless of the fact that I was no longer taking those actions. Consequences, I was learning, had a way of playing out on their own timeline.

The consequences of leaving Colorado were both legal and relational, and in order to return to the state to visit my daughter in the fall of 2005, I had to figure out how to save up enough money to buy a plane ticket to Denver while also saving up enough money to hire a criminal defense attorney in Summit County, where I had lived, to deal with my outstanding warrant. They both seemed like herculean tasks. My credit was shot from years of not paying bills, which made paying for anything without cash next to impossible, and even though I had a steady paycheck, there wasn't much left over to save after I satisfied my obligations. I squirreled away whatever I could spare, though—ten dollars here, twenty dollars there—and in a couple of months I had a few hundred dollars, which meant I could at least start researching attorneys.

After work one day, I walked into the gym and Andrea met me at the door. "Hey," she said, "I've been waiting for you. Let's chat in my office real quick." I wasn't sure what she wanted, but I followed her to the office, which was lined with boxes of Bally's branded T-shirts, and once inside, she shut the door behind us. She walked over to her backpack, which was sitting on her desk chair, and pulled out a manila folder. She opened it and handed me a small piece of paper. "I want you to have this." I took the paper from her hand and immediately realized what it was: a voucher for a plane ticket. I looked up at her, confused. "What is this? I can't take this." Andrea smiled, returned the manila folder to her backpack, and set it on the floor. "Look, I've got this voucher from a trip I never ended up taking, and it expires at the end of this year. I'm not going to use it and I want you to have it. Go see your daughter, Tim. Go to Colorado and make things right with her."

My eyes began to fill as I stood there in the office of this woman I'd known for only a few months, in the basement gym of a high-rise in Chicago's Loop, six months removed from the selfish life I'd been living since I'd moved home from Colorado. I felt I didn't deserve Andrea's generosity in the same way I didn't deserve Dempsey's, and I couldn't understand why she was helping me, why she was extending me this kindness.

"I can't take this," I said, my voice soft and unsure, knowing that I desperately needed it. The voucher, the ticket—it could change everything.

"Yes, you can," she said. "And you will." Andrea smiled and stepped toward me, putting her hands on my shoulders. She gave them a squeeze. "Look, Tim, I want to do this and it just makes sense. Take the voucher. Get the ticket. Go see your kid. It's not complicated."

I stared down at the voucher, which I was holding in my two hands like a stretched-out twenty-dollar bill. I still needed to hire an attorney. I still needed to clear up my warrant. I still needed to make peace with my daughter's mother and make sure she was really okay with me visiting. But a plane ticket made all of that possible in a way that it hadn't been just moments before. The voucher I held in my hand meant that I could see my daughter before the end of the year, something even my counselors in rehab couldn't have predicted. I could finally see how big she'd grown and listen to her laugh and ask her about school and tell her how much I'd missed her, how much I loved her, how sorry I was for leaving. A plane ticket meant that the amends that seemed hardest, if not impossible, to make—with my daughter and my daughter's mother—could now at least be attempted.

"I don't know what to say," I said, my eyes wet with tears even as I tried to hide them.

"Then don't say anything, Tim." Andrea pulled me into a hug. "I'm just glad that I can do this for you."

I closed my eyes. In the background, I heard weights slamming against the floor, and weights slamming against themselves, and footsteps running on a treadmill. I heard people talking and music filtering in through the speakers. And in that small basement office, in the stillness of that hug, I felt the undeniable dynamics of motion, of my recovery moving forward, propelled, once again, by someone who saw something in me that I'd yet to see in myself.

FIVE

I knew something was happening at work when I saw more and more people in nice suits and polished shoes walking by my cubicle and into Dempsey's office. He seemed to be having more meetings than usual, and I'd seen one man in particular—an older man with thin white hair who wore a different flashy pinstriped suit and floral tie every time he visited—four or five times over the course of a couple of weeks.

When I asked Dempsey about it, he was matter-of-fact, but his eyes showed just how excited he actually was. "I'm selling the company, but it's a calculated move that's going to let us take this thing to the next level." Dempsey paused, staring down the hallway, a small smile on his face. "I always said I'd be a millionaire by fifty." He looked at me. "I can't believe it's actually going to happen."

I'd heard stories about how Dempsey had started the business out of his garage, answering a landline telephone he'd placed on a thrift-store desk on the oil-stained concrete floor. He was self-made and self-funded, at least in the early days, using street smarts and a "forgiveness versus permission" mentality to strategically maneuver his way into rooms most people with his background wouldn't have been able to get into. For me to know those stories and see him standing in a tailored suit in a downtown Chicago office, with the promise of a multimillion-dollar deal on the horizon, made it seem like anything was possible, like grit and tenacity and a fierce belief in oneself could make anything happen.

"So what's that mean for us?" I asked.

Dempsey shifted his weight and put his arm on the wall of my cubicle. "Charlotte."

"Charlotte?"

"Yep. The company acquiring us is headquartered in Charlotte. I'm going to move down there. You should too." He smiled and put his giant hand on my shoulder then squeezed it, hard. "I want you there, Tim."

The resistance inside me manifested in my stomach like a runner's cramp. I thought about my life, about the new sober life I was just beginning to build. I had recently moved out of the apartment I shared with Richie and into a small apartment of my own, an environment I could completely control and keep free from substances and temptations. I felt safe and there was finally some consistency, some predictability, in the world I was creating. I'd also fallen even more deeply in love with the city of Chicago. AA meetings in rooms high above the never-quiet streets, nightly walks past the regal Salem limestone greystones in River North, riding the El as it weaved between buildings, hitting the gym after work and breaking a sweat, folding clothes, ironing dress shirts, reading paperback legal thrillers on park benches near the river over lunch—small acts of normalcy that were altogether uneventful, but somehow incredibly meaningful. They were indicators of progress in my life, small reassurances that I was on the right path and moving in the right direction. I was finding a sense of contentment with myself and my city, and I didn't want to leave Chicago. I sure as shit didn't want to move to Charlotte, a place I'd only been to once.

"Can I think about it?" I asked.

Dempsey's smile faded and he pulled his hand off my shoulder. "What's there to fucking think about?"

"It's just that . . ." I paused, all the words I wanted to say stuck in my throat. Dempsey would never understand the way I felt, and it seemed futile to try to explain it. He phrased it as a question, but it was clear to me that it wasn't a request. There was no way I could say no to him. Not after all that had happened. Not after rehab. Not after all that he had done for me. As I stood there in that hallway before the man who had changed my life in ways large and small, I knew before our conversation was over that my agreement was nothing more than a formality. Chicago was out. Charlotte was in. All that was left was to pack up and move.

Before I left the city I loved, before I held a small going-away party at a bar near my apartment, before I broke my lease in Chicago, packed up a U-Haul with all my possessions, and drove to a high-rise in Charlotte's South End neighborhood, I returned to Colorado. I'd saved up just enough money to hire a Colorado-based criminal defense attorney, who was working on getting my warrant quashed, and the day I landed at Denver International Airport was the exact day the judge was set to rule on the case. If the warrant was quashed, I would likely owe some sort of fine and possibly have to complete community service, but I wouldn't be arrested. However, if the judge ruled the other way and the warrant wasn't quashed, it would remain active until I either turned myself in or encountered the police, who, I was told by my attorney, would have no choice but to arrest me.

I knew I was doing the right thing, but I was anxious about doing it. I couldn't get the thought out of my head that when I deplaned in Colorado, a battalion of police officers would swarm me at the gate, guns drawn, and tell me to put my hands behind my head and lie on the floor face down. It wasn't rational, and I'd likely seen too many movies, but I'd been arrested so many times in the past, and so many of those arrests had been in Colorado, that I couldn't shake the thought from my mind.

When I landed, I called my attorney—heart pounding, palms sweating—and she told me that the news was good and the judge had ruled in my favor. As of that morning, the warrant was no longer active. I had fines to pay, she said, and some counseling to complete, but I could visit my daughter without any sort of legal repercussions. "Congrats," she said as I pulled my suitcase through the terminal. "Now go have fun. The hard stuff is over."

The hard stuff was far from over, but the quashed warrant felt like a sign, an affirmation that all the sacrifices I'd been making and the sober life I'd been pursuing were finally yielding results in real, meaningful ways. I was moments away from walking out the doors of Baggage Claim, where the daughter I hadn't seen in five years would suddenly pull up in a car. She'd be five years older than the last time I saw her. Five years taller. Five years from who she was when I last held her in my arms.

I stood in the airport that day, a bead of sweat over my upper lip, second guessing the outfit I wore, hyperaware of my surroundings, of the way I looked, of the way I felt, scared and unsure, because what does a person say or do in a moment like that? How does a person, how does a father, ask for forgiveness for abandoning their child?

I walked into the cool Colorado air pulling a cheap Rollaboard suitcase while airbrakes from rental-car buses hissed and people pulled ski poles and mountain bikes from the backs of SUVs, and an old Buick sedan drove up and stopped right in front of me. I recognized my ex in the front seat, and I smiled at her, and she smiled back, and I couldn't believe that we were seeing each other again after so much had happened, after all the fights and all the arrests and all the drugs, two people who were both different and the same, changed by the years that had passed since we were together, altered by time, healed in some ways, but still very much aware that nothing had been resolved between us, and that maybe nothing ever would be. I was so nervous to be there, to be in the same place as she was, and then the back door opened and my daughter jumped out as if she had practiced the move a million times before, opening the door with one hand while swinging her legs out and launching herself onto the pavement, where she landed and began running in one smooth movement. I could see in that moment that she was a born athlete, that she could navigate landscapes with purpose and ease and grace, and she ran toward me as if she'd been waiting for this moment for as long as I had.

I squatted down to meet her and pulled her into my arms and against my chest. She felt warm and soft and real, and she smelled like Fruit Roll-Ups, or maybe gummy worms, and her arms were around my neck, and they were squeezing me, and I was completely and utterly shattered by her hug. And even though I knew nothing had yet been fixed, and nothing had yet been said, and so much would have to be figured out between us, it was the beginning of something new, something I could never have anticipated, even back when I was in rehab, and for the moment it was enough.

When I got back to the office after my trip, I told Dempsey about my visit. I told him how my daughter had shown me the school she attended, and how she could jump off a curb on her inline skates just like I used to do, and how we both ate pizza and candy until our bellies ached. I told him how we laughed until there were tears in our eyes and how I couldn't take my eyes off her the entire time I was there, how I studied every freckle on her perfectly tanned skin, how leaving her to get on the plane felt like a criminal act.

Dempsey listened as he always did, with a cigar in his hand, a swirl of smoke crawling toward the ceiling, papers strewn about his desk. "Looks like you're going to have to find some business to attend to in Colorado," he said after I finished talking, blowing a funnel of cigar smoke into the air as I sat across from him in a red leather chair. He paused and watched the smoke dissipate. "Shit, maybe we'll even open a Denver office at some point."

"Wait," I said. "What are you talking about?" We'd never discussed opening an office in Denver, and I'd never known him to do a lot of business in Colorado.

Dempsey looked at me and then leaned back in his chair, staring up and out the windows behind me. "I don't know. We'll see about the office. It might make sense at some point, though. But in the meantime, find ways to get to Colorado. Book layovers there on your business trips. When you're flying home from the West Coast, fly through Denver. Fuck it. Get creative." He took a pull from his Padron and exhaled. He smiled. "It's time for you to be a dad, Tim. Do what you need to do. Your daughter needs you. This much I know."

I leaned back in my chair and caught Dempsey's eye. "Thanks, Sean. I don't even know what to say."

He smiled again and put his cigar on the ashtray. "Don't mention it," he said, and he swiveled his chair toward the computer next to him and put his hands on the keyboard. "Now get the fuck out of here. I got shit to do."

I laughed and stood. "Catch you later," I said and walked out of his office and back to my cubicle, where I sat down and started searching for flights back to Denver.

SIX

The highest highs and the lowest lows were braided together in those years I worked for Dempsey, and they tethered me to him in a way that felt permanent. His generosity and kindness toward me were unexpected and unprecedented, and they cemented in me a deep sense of gratitude and loyalty, and a fierce desire to please him. He made me feel like I was smart, and like I belonged in the business world, and like I mattered in a way I'd never experienced before. He made me feel like I was more than just a high-school dropout with a long criminal record. According to Dempsey, I could actually become something. Or, more accurately, I actually *was* something already.

Dempsey had introduced me to a mesmerizing world I had previously seen only in movies. He showed me New York City and Miami, Los Angeles and Austin, New Orleans and Las Vegas. He showed me the Ace Hotel and the Ritz Carlton and the Four Seasons. He showed me room service and dry-aged steaks and airport clubs and first-class seats; and once, when we had meetings lined up in a number of different cities in California, he took me on a private jet that flew us to small airports I'd never heard of where black SUVs picked us up, brought us to our meetings, and then brought us back to the plane again.

But as unbelievably generous as he was, there was that other side of him, the "fire-breathing dragon" as he called it, the side of him that could make my adrenaline flow and hands tremble by raising his voice and slamming his fist onto the boardroom table, a hint of physical violence ever-present in the air. There was that side of him that could make a flight attendant cry, or get him thrown off an airplane, or cause him to knock a slow-moving man sideways with his suitcase as he passed him in the airport. There was that side of him that got us tossed out of restaurants and hotels for exploding on the staff. There was that side of him that was full of dragon fire ready to be unleashed, the side that was always moments away from burning the city to the ground.

When Dempsey exploded on me, which happened almost weekly, his voice rising and his jaw setting in anger, it was often not long after he had done something generous for me, and I felt a mix of fear, rage, embarrassment, confusion, and cowardice. Regardless of what he was mad about, and regardless of whether his perception was right or wrong, I was never allowed to explain myself—none of us who worked with him were—so we just had to take it, to sit there as he spit venom, each insult designed for maximum impact. I'd leave his presence after getting screamed at, seething, feeling angry and weak for not speaking up for myself, for not defending myself, for not forcing him to hear my side. I'd leave his presence feeling like less of a man, unsure of who I was, like the fuck-up I had so often felt like when I was younger.

Later, I'd replay the day's events in my mind, thinking about what Dempsey had said to me during his latest eruption, rehearsing all the lines I wished I'd said, all the comebacks I'd thought of since, and I'd go to the gym and spend my workout thinking not about how much I hated him, but that I deserved every bit of it. If I wasn't such a fuck-up, I'd think, if I wasn't such a shitty employee and a bad father and a terrible son, then maybe I wouldn't be yelled at so much and Dempsey wouldn't be forced to treat me the way he did. He probably didn't want to fuck with me as much as he did, I'd think, but my inability to perform at a high level, to be a real man, made it so he didn't have a choice. Maybe if I simply worked harder and made fewer mistakes, he wouldn't be so disappointed in me.

On those days when he had laid into me in the same unrelenting way men on construction sites had when I was younger, when I was skinny and even more unsure of myself, I'd lie flat on the weight bench at the gym, hands wrapped around the barbell, a forty-five and twenty-five-pound plate on each side, and press the weights up over and over again until my chest and shoulders screamed in protest. I'd get on the treadmill and sprint a mile as fast as I could, sweat flying off me and landing on the control panel, blurring the digital numbers, my arms pumping and my chest heaving, until I completed the mile and nearly collapsed on the treadmill, welcoming the pain as penance. Deep down I knew I couldn't change the way Dempsey came at me, the way he saw me, the way he exploited my weaknesses, but I could transform my body, I could become bigger and stronger and more violent, I could inhabit more space. I could work to eradicate the fear I felt in those moments when I was being screamed at by a bigger, tougher man by becoming a bigger, tougher man.

I was eating a sandwich in the office lunchroom one day when Dempsey walked in and sat down next to me. He began talking about an employee he was frustrated with for one reason or another, a man who was good at his work but also not "man" enough in Dempsey's eyes. "He's never even been in a street fight," he said to me, shaking his head in disgust. "Can you fucking believe it?"

I could, of course, believe it, because not engaging in fights on the street is a rational and normal way to live, but I couldn't do anything but agree because I knew that in Dempsey's world, and also in mine at the time, masculinity was a status that needed to be earned over and over again—through strength, through hostility, through violence.

I didn't have the words back then, or the perspective, or even the inclination, to challenge how I thought about masculinity, but I do now, and I can see how so much of my experience with Dempsey was driven by my desire to "be a man," even though, as a concept, as a construct, masculinity was something I thought about exactly zero times in my twenties.

Or perhaps what I mean is just the opposite—that I thought about masculinity nonstop, without ever knowing that masculinity was what I was thinking about.

In those years with Dempsey, I didn't understand that there could be masculinities, plural, instead of masculinity, singular. I didn't understand that I could define myself as a man however I wanted to, or that I could simply define myself as a person, without ascribing a gender label to it. I didn't have to live in a one-dimensional, archetypal version of a man that, if I was being honest with myself, I knew I really hadn't fit into to begin with.

Growing up as the stepson of a heavy-equipment operator whose hands were always calloused and whose work was largely defined by physical labor and physical toughness, I absorbed and tried to emulate what I saw around me. I knew that a man worked, and he worked incredibly hard, and he didn't complain, no matter how badly something hurt, no matter how tired he got, no matter what circumstances arose. I knew a man put his head down and his feelings aside. Or, better yet, he buried them completely.

As I grew into my late teens, and then later, in the Dempsey years, no matter how hard I tried, I found that I could never quite fit into that traditional masculinity mold. I was too emotional, too soft, too concerned with feelings. I cried too easily, and felt too much, and was never quite tough enough. Worst of all, I lacked the "killer instinct" that real men had, that ability to fight at a moment's notice, to stand my ground with my chest out, unafraid, and throw hands when the situation demanded it.

However, that didn't stop me from trying. When I looked at Dempsey, I could see all the ways in which he was flawed, but I could also see all the ways in which he was a better man than me, all the ways he was tougher and rougher and more dominant. I wanted to be like that, to be like him, to be a man that other men looked up to. Or better yet, feared.

"Work harder. Be tougher. Shut the fuck up and get shit done." That was my internal dialogue—as well as the external dialogue I often heard from Dempsey—and it was relentless. Even all these years later, it's still the most common refrain I have in my head. Which isn't to say that it's the wrong refrain, or that the refrain itself is bad. It's simply that I've come to understand that these qualities—toughness, hard work, determination, grit—have nothing to do with masculinity whatsoever. They're simply qualities, and they're available for anyone to inhabit should they decide that they want to.

In the books and essays I would read about masculinity in the years after Dempsey, I would finally begin to understand and appreciate that I had agency in how I perceived myself, and in how I showed up in the world—and in the type of man I wanted to be. I would come to realize that I could inhabit a far different and more nuanced type of masculinity, one that was more aware and more considerate and more expansive—and yes, more emotional. I would come to realize that the man I was could be different in every way from the man he was, and that over time, I could redefine the way I thought about masculinity completely.

And yet, I would be remiss if I didn't also say this. While Dempsey embodied a toxic masculinity that was problematic on nearly every level, the irony I've come to believe is that Dempsey's toxicity and rage were—in large and substantial ways, at least in those early years—responsible for my sobriety. I've come to believe that I was too hard-headed and too rebellious and too deep in the cycle of drinking and using and partying to have responded to anything less than pure aggression from someone bigger and stronger and angrier than me. It was almost as if he were a sort of chemotherapy for my alcoholism and addiction—a powerful medicine that eradicated the cancer inside me but slowly poisoned me in the process. That doesn't make what he did right. But it was effective nonetheless. And as in all complicated relationships, I've learned to live inside the complexity.

I turned up at the front desk of a boxing gym in Charlotte not long after moving. It was an old Lenscrafters that had been renovated by a couple of pro fighters who were a few years past their careers, and it had rows of eighty-pound heavy bags hanging from a steel frame, a wrestling mat tucked into a corner, and a boxing ring set up right in the center of the gym. It smelled like gym clothes and sweat and bodies, and I fell in love with it the moment I walked in.

I began showing up at the gym every day after work and on the weekends, with sixteen-ounce gloves and a tangled mess of sweaty hand wraps, taking group classes that focused on jumping rope and shadow boxing, and working with a trainer who began teaching me the fundamentals of fighting. Over time, I learned how to sit comfortably in my boxing stance—feet staggered, left foot angled in front of the right, light on my toes—and move laterally without crossing my feet. I learned how to turn over a punch, how to slip and weave and pivot, how to create angles by stepping off to the side after throwing a one-two combination. Perhaps most importantly, I learned how to breathe, how to exhale sharply as I threw a punch so my diaphragm would tighten, flexed and ready in case it had to contend with a counterpunch to the body. I began to see that boxing was so much more than throwing punches. It was strategic and cerebral, and there was a level of sophistication to it, an elegance, a discipline that I'd never encountered in any other sport.

Early in my time there, during one of the evening classes, just after we'd finished fifteen minutes of jump rope and pulled our gloves on, my trainer, a short, muscular 140-pounder in his midtwenties named Kali, had us partner up. "You're going to learn how to parry jabs tonight," he yelled to the group over the ever-present hip-hop playlist. "Find a partner who's about your size and square off, close enough that your jab can land. One of you will throw ten jabs while the other parries them, and then you'll switch."

I knew that parrying a jab meant using my glove to misdirect the punch, and that it was a fundamental defensive move in boxing. I swiveled my head and locked eyes with a guy across the gym who looked to be a bit bigger and longer than me, and we partnered up. To start, he was on offense, and I was on defense. Kali gave us the signal to begin, and I watched for his body to move, for his body to hint that a punch was coming. When it did, it came more quickly than I'd anticipated, and I felt the sting as his jab cracked me across the nose. He smiled and I wiped a drop of sweat off my forehead with my glove and sat back in my stance, gloves up near my chin, ready for the next one. He stepped forward and fired. Again, the jab landed squarely across my nose. I couldn't seem to figure out the timing, or the distance, or the movement—or anything, for that matter. I glanced around the room, embarrassed and frustrated, and saw all the other fighters firing jabs at one another, successfully parrying punches just like Kali had showed us. I looked back at my partner and got ready. He snapped off another jab and again I mistimed it, my nose now tingling with pain. Kali was suddenly next to us, animated. "Either move your fucking head or parry the jab, Tim. For Christ's sake, you know the damn punch is coming. Quit overthinking it."

I got back in my stance and waited. The jab came and this time I parried it, but it felt awkward and erratic. "Good," Kali said. "Now make your movement even smaller. Don't exaggerate it. Boxing is all about small adjustments. Take in the information. Then make an adjustment. Now do it again."

My partner fired off another jab, and then another, and then another, and some of them I parried and some of them I didn't, and soon I was dripping sweat and breathing hard through my mouthpiece.

Later, as I sat on the mat pulling off my hand wraps, replaying every single punch I had taken, pressing my finger on the bridge of my nose where it stung, frustrated with myself, sweat dripping into a small pool between my legs, Kali came up and sat down next to me. "Look, man," he said, leaning back on his hands. "Don't be too hard on yourself. Everyone has days like this."

I stared at the puddle of sweat between my legs and watched as it slowly got bigger. I was incredibly frustrated with myself, unable to let it go. "It's like I just couldn't figure it out. Like I had brain fog or something."

"Yeah, but Tim, here's what you need to understand. This shit takes time, and even more than that it takes repetition. We drill the fundamentals over and over because the fundamentals are the most important tools you have. It doesn't matter how strong you are, or how tough you are, because if you don't have the fundamentals, if you can't parry a jab or tuck your elbows to your sides, if you can't bring your punches back to your chin after you throw them, you're going to pay a price. Maybe not today. Maybe not next week. But at some point, you're going to wake up on a canvas wondering what the fuck just happened."

I nodded but didn't say anything, thinking about how everything he was saying could apply to sobriety too. Don't drink, go to meetings. Those were the fundamentals of sobriety, and the power came from their repetition.

"There's the other thing you need to know, Tim. Boxing is math. It's arithmetic. It's addition and subtraction. You ever think about why punches are numbered? I do. And I have a theory. A one-two combo. A one-two-three. You add them up and you get a number and that number is how good you are. You're only ever as good as the sum total of the number of punches you've thrown and the number of punches you've taken. You just started, right? You're maybe a thousand punches good at this point. Imagine what you're going to be like when you've thrown ten thousand punches. And seen ten thousand coming at you. Or thirty thousand. Or a hundred thousand. Sure, you took punches today that you didn't need to take. But you learned, right? You felt that sting, right? That's what it's all about, Tim. Accepting the math and learning from it." He paused and looked around the gym, which had emptied out except for the guy I had been paired up with, who was still hitting the heavy bag, his punches landing with a rhythmic slap. The music was still on, but it was lowered, and Kali was able to talk without straining to be heard. "Look, man, boxing isn't easy. And it's not for everybody. But it'll change you. It'll change the way you see the world." He looked at me and I picked my head up and met his gaze. "It'll also change the way you see yourself."

I looked down at the pool of sweat between my legs and used my forefinger to draw a line through it. I was struck by what Kali had just said—this idea of seeing myself in new ways. It seemed like that's what I had been doing since I'd met Dempsey, since I'd left rehab: reconstructing my sense of self and beginning to see myself differently. First as an employee, then as a sober person, then as a father, now as a fighter. I could feel that there was some sort of visceral connection between boxing and sobriety, but I couldn't yet put my finger on exactly what it was, and it would be years before I truly understood it, before I understood how intertwined it all was, how fighting in the ring and fighting to become a different person, a different man, were nearly the same thing.

"Thanks, Kali," I said. "I hope so."

He stood up and brushed off his rear end. "See you tomorrow?"

I grabbed my hand wraps and started to roll them up. "You know it, man. See you then."

By the fall of 2007, I'd been living in Charlotte for a couple of months, and it was an adjustment I was having a tough time with. It was a new city in a new part of the country where I knew no one, and even though Dempsey invited me over for dinner often and did what he could to make me feel welcome in Charlotte, I was lonely. I missed Chicago and the sober community I had just started to build there. I missed the basement gym and the smell of the wind blowing off the lake and hearing the low whir of the El Train as I made my morning coffee. More than anything, though, I missed the feeling of contentment I had just begun to feel. The feeling of belonging I had just begun to identify.

I knew enough about recovery at that point in my journey to know that loneliness could be treacherous for sobriety, so I set out to find an AA meeting in Charlotte that I could begin attending regularly. I quickly found a place called the Triangle Club, a large building on a small piece of property dedicated entirely to recovery meetings. I began showing up at the Triangle Club almost every night, falling into the predictable rhythm and structure of AA meetings. I sometimes got there early and made coffee, or helped move chairs around between meetings, but I mostly just showed up in the evenings after work, found a seat in the corner, my coffee steaming in a small Styrofoam cup, and listened to men and women share stories about "what it was like, what happened, and what it's like now."

Looking back I can see that, in so many ways, small decisions like these, like attending meetings at the Triangle Club and finding a sober community to be a part of, saved me from relapsing in those early years. I knew that I wanted to be sober badly, and that I wanted to inhabit a different kind of life, but I was very much alone in my recovery. My parents, my friends back in Chicago—none of them knew, really, where I was or what I was doing, and it would have been so easy to go back to my old life, to my old ways of thinking and being. After all, who would have known?

In the years after Charlotte, after Dempsey, people would often ask me how I did it, how I managed to achieve long-term sobriety when so many others fail. I mostly wouldn't have any answer for them. I mostly wouldn't know what to say. Because sobriety, like a book, is simply an attempt—an attempt to make something new from something old, to make meaning from what once seemed to lack any sort of meaning at all.

For Dempsey, Charlotte was the Promised Land.

After his company sold and the money had been transferred—rumors were that he'd pocketed more than ten million dollars—Dempsey boarded a plane for North Carolina with a carry-on suitcase and simply never came back. He filed for divorce from Summer—she and Dempsey had been living in separate houses by then, Summer in the beautiful home they had built years before and Dempsey in a small brown house on a wooded piece of land ten minutes away from her—and immediately began a romantic relationship with a recently divorced single mom who was a year older than me. He bought a stunning mansion on a picturesque piece of land in a wealthy part of Charlotte, and it was a rags-to-riches story if I ever did see one, filled with all the expected clichés.

On one of my trips back to Chicago, maybe two or three months after Dempsey had left for Charlotte, he asked if I would hire movers to pack up the small brown house he had been living in. "I need you to get all the stuff in that house together and have it sent here," he said. "I'm done with that place." I heard a match strike in the background and imagined him taking a long pull from his cigar. "Now that I think of it, I don't have a fucking clue where the house key is. Break a window if you have to. Just get me my shit."

I arranged to have movers meet me at the property on a gray Saturday morning, and I showed up early to figure out a way in. It was quiet and cold when I pulled up, the trees that lined the property were bare except for a few brown leaves that clung to their branches, and I located an unlocked window around the back of the house and climbed in to find that the heat was on full blast, the smell of stale cigar smoke and unwashed dishes hovering over every surface in the house.

Dempsey had been driving a rental car and living in a Charlotte hotel while the details of his real estate transaction came together, and he hadn't been back to his little brown house for months. Unread newspapers were piled up on the lawn, dirty dishes were piled up in the sink, half-smoked cigars were piled up in ashtrays, and it looked as if Dempsey had indeed walked out and vanished one day without warning or notice.

When the movers arrived, I let them inside and they scanned the room, taking in the mess, and looked at me quizzically. "If it's not obviously garbage, pack it in a box," I said. "Pretty much everything in this place goes." The movers got to work wrapping everything in packing paper, and four hours later the house was empty and the moving truck was pulling away. I walked through the now-empty house, checking each room one last time before I left, and I couldn't shake the feeling that the universe was trying to teach me some sort of lesson about hastily cleaned-up messes and half-ass solutions. I pulled my cell phone out of my pocket and walked to a window that looked out onto the woods that lined the back of the property. Squirrels chased each other around and up the trees, jumping from branch to branch, frolicking, and I dialed Dempsey's number.

"Good to go?" he said.

"Yep. The movers just left. Should be arriving at your new place in a few days."

One of the squirrels had broken off from the chase and was now searching the grass near the bottom of a tree. I watched it as it stopped searching and sat back on its legs, its front paws holding an acorn like a corn cob, spinning and munching.

"Thanks for handling all of that," Dempsey said. "I really appreciate it."

I turned from the window and walked back into the living room. I'd turned the heat off and the house was much colder than when I'd walked in earlier. I shivered and zipped up my jacket, took one last look around to see if I'd missed anything, and started for the door.

"Not a problem," I said. "I'll see you when I get back."

We said goodbye and I slipped the phone into the back pocket of my jeans. I stepped into the cold November air, pulling the door shut behind me, and started for the car. The air smelled like wet leaves and asphalt, like home, and I wanted nothing more than to stay there and breathe the crisp, cold air of the geography I knew.

The fissure between Dempsey and me emerged and began to propagate not long after I had arrived in Charlotte. I had tried to make the best of my situation, even going as far as using the few thousand dollars I'd managed to save up while paying off my debt as a down payment on a condo at the tail end of 2007, thinking that if I "put down roots" in North Carolina I would feel better about where I lived, but I was resentful about being forced to leave Chicago. As much as I had tried to deny my growing antipathy, and to focus on how grateful I was to Dempsey for all he had done for me, and to distract myself with boxing and AA meetings, I could no longer deny my geographic frustration. Since moving, I had felt trapped and out of options, and all I could think about was how the life I had always wanted to live was waiting for me in Chicago. And yet here I was, in Charlotte, spinning my wheels in a city I didn't know and didn't want to be in.

By early 2008, three years sober and with a life that was different in every conceivable way from the one I'd led when I met Dempsey in Baker's Square, I'd begun to understand the fundamental challenge of my situation. While it was true that I'd gotten sober and resolved the last of my legal problems, and I'd become a different sort of person altogether, perhaps even a businessman in some respects, I still lacked a college degree or formal training in business and finance. I enjoyed the considerable benefits of being Dempsey's Guy—the nice dinners, the travel, the higher-than-average salary— but I had begun to realize that if Dempsey wasn't in the picture, if I left Dempsey's company and applied for another job in finance, I would be underqualified for just about every single position except for an entry-level one. I was wearing the proverbial Golden Handcuffs, a phrase I'd once heard someone in the office use. I realized that without Dempsey, I was just a Baker's Square waiter who had traded the restaurant for the cubicle.

"Chicago's off the fucking table," Dempsey said, clearly annoyed that I was bringing it up yet again. "If you don't fucking like Charlotte, then you can move to Baltimore with Steven, but you're not moving back to Chicago. End of story."

I wanted to reach through the phone and strangle Dempsey. I'd asked him on numerous occasions if I could move back to Chicago, where we still had an office, and there didn't seem to be any obvious business reason why I couldn't. I traveled a fair amount of the time, and the location of my home office seemed to be form over function. I could fulfill all my responsibilities from Chicago—or from anywhere, for that matter—just the same as I could fulfill them from Charlotte. It just didn't make any fucking sense to me.

"So, Chicago's off the table but Baltimore isn't?"

"Yeah."

I squeezed my eyes shut as hard as I could and held them closed for a few seconds. When I opened them, I watched the pixels slowly merge back together.

Dempsey had recently hired a man named Steven to run the risk management department of the company, and as part of Steven's employment package, he had been allowed to stay in his home city of Baltimore and open an office there. Baltimore wasn't Chicago, but it wasn't Charlotte either, and it would put some distance between Dempsey and me, which I definitely needed.

"Fine," I said. "Fuck it. Baltimore it is."

I found a renter for my condo in Charlotte and, in March of 2008, moved to Baltimore, where I hastily—and, I would soon learn, foolishly—bought a condo in a neighborhood called Reservoir Hill. I didn't have much money to put down—a few thousand dollars at most—and rates were high, but it didn't matter because I think that, in some ways, I was trying to trick myself into feeling better about who I was. After all, I reasoned, if I owned two pieces of real estate and drove a nice car, even if I was house-broke and cash-poor, I couldn't possibly be the same person I had been just a few years before.

Situated in West Baltimore, just off the Jones Falls Expressway, Reservoir Hill was filled with late-nineteenth- and early-twentieth-century row houses, with some blocks completely restored and others completely abandoned. I had bought my small condo sight unseen, but it was in a newly renovated hundred-year-old brick building, on a quiet street called Park Avenue, which I found amusing, because I associated it with the ritzy street in New York and it was anything but. Baltimore felt different from Chicago in a lot of ways, but similar too, since they were both working-class cities made up of neighborhoods. Reservoir Hill was diverse and filled with city workers and public-school officials, teachers and mechanics, college professors and grade-school principals, and it boasted endless lines of brick-and-Formstone-faced rowhomes that were occasionally interrupted by ornate Victorian mansions, crumbling and in various states of disarray, but beautiful to look at nonetheless.

Just as I had in Charlotte, when I got to Baltimore, I found a boxing gym and an AA meeting. Soon after moving, I was spending my evenings and weekends talking with other alcoholics in rooms that smelled of cheap coffee and cigarette smoke, or at the gym snapping off jabs and right hands as a way of exorcising the demons inside me.

I'd been boxing for a little over a year by then, and I found an almost indescribable mixture of joy and fear in the sport—and those two feelings had somehow melded together and placed an intoxicating hold on me. In the year-plus that I'd been boxing, I'd gotten better and found my footwork, and I began sparring as often as I could, moving around the canvas with more confidence, slipping and catching punches, countering, learning how to stand my ground in the center of the ring.

I was also beginning to see just how important boxing had become to my recovery. It had unexpectedly given me a portal into my truest self, into the parts of me that I liked the least. My constant fear of failure, my anger, the ways in which I had tried to manipulate people, the hurt I'd caused—I suddenly had to confront all of it. There were no distractions in the boxing gym, no phones to look at, not a computer in sight. So I threw punches at the heavy bag one after another, sweat dripping down my face and chest, breathing hard, alone with my thoughts, knowing something was happening inside of me but not knowing exactly what that something was.

On days that I sparred, I had to force myself to accept the fear I felt and move past it, to move toward the fight, toward the danger, to keep my wits about me as punches came, hard and with intention. In the ring there was no hiding from what I felt or whom I faced. There was nowhere to go and nothing to do except to accept the moment for what it was and feel what I was feeling. It was the most stripped down I had ever been, even more than in rehab. It was there that I was the most vulnerable, which is to say the most human.

In so many ways, my time inside the ring replicated my time inside sobriety. In Baltimore, I had once again found myself alone in a new city where I had to fend for myself, where I had to rely on the fundamentals I'd learned in rehab and in AA meetings, the sharing and the showing up, the jabs and right hands of recovery. In the time since I'd left Chicago and moved to Charlotte, and then from Charlotte to Baltimore, I'd also continued working to establish a relationship with my daughter. I'd flown back to Colorado a dozen times since our first visit, since that first day I'd watched her emerge from the back seat of that Buick, but the novelty of me being back in her life had worn off and the real work of establishing a relationship strained by geographical distance had started. She was asking questions about why I left and why I wouldn't move there to be with her, and the answers I gave, which were real and valid to me, seemed more like convenient excuses to her. Who was I to tell her otherwise? To complicate things even more, her mother and I weren't seeing eye to eye, and Dempsey and I weren't seeing eye to eye, and the work of staying sober had begun to feel not unlike the work of staying in shape. I was tired—tired from flying around the country and navigating the ever-revolving cannon of anger Dempsey aimed at me. Tired from trying to convince my daughter how much I loved her. Tired of trying to be a version of myself I still couldn't define.

Baltimore, which the guys in the boxing gym called "B'more" or "Mobtown," is a storied fight town, a gritty, steely blue-collar city that once watched with pride as local fighter Hasim "The Rock" Rahman, in one of boxing's biggest upsets, knocked out Lenox Lewis in 2001 to win the unified heavyweight championship of the world. Rahman was only five years older than me, and I knew the story and had rewatched the fight online before I moved there, and by the time I was living in Baltimore, Rahman's son was on the come up in the young amateur boxing circuit.

One night as I moved around the double-end bag, tossing off jabs and right hands while working on head movement, Rahman showed up with his son so he could get some work in with another young fighter. I'd learned that unlike other professional sports, like basketball or football, boxing was a sport where amateurs and pros were often in the same place, working on the same things.

Boxing—when it was stripped down—was about showing up and putting in work, over and over, day after day. And because I knew that, and because I showed up and put in work day after day, I felt more like a fighter than I ever had before. Even my body had transformed: I was a lean and muscular 185 pounds, with a nice right hand and a decent left hook.

The gym that I trained at was in a suburb about thirty minutes outside of the city, not far from the office I had transferred to. I had a trainer named Rodney James, a retired journeyman fighter a few years older than me with a square jaw and a quiet disposition. We began working together in the evenings when I was in town and not traveling for work, moving around the canvas together as he held mitts, drilling the fundamentals and sharpening my toolset. Rodney wanted to build off my natural gifts—athleticism and strength—and teach me how to use them to my advantage. "Slip, and then counter," he would say during our sessions, firing a jab at my nose and preparing to catch my counter right hand. "Move that head, and then sit down on that punch."

I often ran in the evenings when I got back from the gym, tired but knowing I had to keep improving my cardiovascular fitness. Boxing was taxing in a way that even the soccer I'd played in my youth hadn't been, so I'd arrive home from my sessions with Rodney, slip on my runners, and head right back out the door, while the sun collapsed on the horizon to the west. I'd jog down Park Avenue to Druid Hill Park, which was nearly the size of Central Park in New York City, and I'd run laps around Druid Lake, counting the times I passed the thirty-foot-tall Moorish Tower, which I'd read was built by George Frederick in 1870 and made of solid marble. I'd rhythmically breathe in the cool night air, hearing only my breath and my footfalls and the occasional siren in the distance, and think about what it must have felt like for Rahman to knock out Lennox Lewis, to do the thing no one thought he could do, to stand there glistening with sweat while looking out at the frenzied crowd, as

Lennox lay on the mat, winning the title he'd dreamed about since he was a kid. I'd think about all that and feel my adrenaline start to surge, because I wanted to do the same thing. Not win the heavyweight title, of course, but to fight in front of a crowd of people and do a thing no one, especially not me, ever thought I would, or could, do. I would think about signing up for the Golden Gloves, the most well-known amateur tournament in boxing, imagining how I would do. I could see myself climbing through the ropes and stepping into the ring, feeling the canvas flex beneath my feet, a crowd of people watching from the bleachers, adrenaline dumping and coursing through me. The thoughts would make me both excited and terrified, and I'd never wanted and not wanted to do something that much in my entire life.

I said as much to Rodney, and he encouraged me to sign up, excited and more than happy to help me obtain a boxing passbook and a physical, the two requirements to compete in a Golden Gloves event. And then just two months after I'd decided to fight, during which I trained as much as I could between work trips, I stood in line the morning of the tournament with dozens of other fighters, waiting to weigh in. I'd signed up to fight at 178 pounds, which seemed reasonable at the time, but after all the training I'd done in the two months leading up to the fight, and all the nerves, I stepped on the scale and watched as my official weight was recorded as 170. I looked around the room, the nervous energy palpable, and felt undertrained and underweight.

When I showed up for the fight later that evening, at the Sugar Ray Leonard Boxing Center in Palmer Park, Maryland, not far from Northwest Stadium, where the Washington Redskins played, I learned that I was the sixteenth and final fight of the night in the novice division. I sat in the bleachers and watched as young men from lighter weight classes fought, trying to calm my nerves, looking around the gym and trying to figure out whom I'd be fighting. When I was two fights out, Rodney pulled me over to the gloves table, where two boxing officials sat and offered us a choice between two sets of gloves. Rodney picked one up and inspected it, feeling its impact point, the stiffness of the leather, and made his choice. "These feel pretty good," he said, glancing at me. "They should have a nice crack to them." I followed Rodney over to a pair of chairs off in one corner of the gym, and he had me sit on one backward-facing chair so he could wrap my hands. "Relax, man," he said, as I rested my wrist on the back of the metal folding chair and he began to methodically wrap gauze around my knuckles. "All you need to do is remember the fundamentals. Use your strength. Throw your punches with bad intentions. Make him feel it every time you let your hands go."

I nodded and watched as Rodney folded the gauze across my knuckles in a "pillow" before wrapping it around my hand and asking me to feel it. "Good?" I punched my right fist into the palm of my left hand and nodded. "Good," I said. Rodney helped me pull my gloves on. "How do you feel?"

"How do I feel? I'm fucking nervous, Rodney," I said, shaking my wrist out. "Fuck, man. Is this normal? What the fuck am I even doing here?"

Rodney laughed. "Hell yeah, it's normal. The nerves are crazy. But you need to get a hold of it, man. Calm yourself. Breathe. Think of it like a sparring session."

I thought back to all the sparring sessions we'd had leading up to this, all the rounds I'd left puddles of sweat on the canvas, all the times I'd showed up to work with black eyes and glove burns on my forehead. I'd put in the work. That much I knew. I'd showed up and I'd taken my licks and now I was here, at this place a thousand miles away from Chicago, in a gym full of people I didn't know, getting ready to step into a ring with a man fifteen pounds heavier than me, to fight for the right to move on to the next round of the tournament. But no matter what Rodney said, no matter how many times he told me to reframe it, and to think about it differently, I couldn't shake my nerves, my lack of confidence. I wanted to pull my gloves off and find my car in the parking lot. Turn over the ignition. Jump on the highway and not look back.

And then before I knew it I was climbing between the ropes, and I could see that all the eyes of all the people in the gym were trained on me, waiting, watching, and it felt like my arms and legs were attached to someone else's body. I could see the man I was about to fight across the ring from me, and he looked calm and collected, ignoring me and walking slowly back and forth, from one side of the ring to the other, as if he'd done this a thousand times before, as if it were indeed another sparring session, and then the bell had rung and we had met in the middle of the ring. I threw a lazy jab and Rodney yelled at me to wake up, to *wake the fuck up*, and I think I heard him but my arms still felt like they belonged to someone else, and my legs felt glued to the canvas. We moved around and I saw a jab come at me and I tried to parry it and then another one came and I felt the crack of a punch landing. It came hard and fast and with intention and, in that moment, I realized that I indeed needed to wake up like Rodney had said, and that I needed to move my head and throw my hands and do all the things we had worked on in the gym. But suddenly another punch landed and I stumbled back into the ropes, and I knew I was in a bad position, against the ropes, and Rodney was yelling and I was scared, the fear pulsing thickly through my bloodstream. I saw another left hook coming and I instinctually ducked and pivoted to my left and off the ropes, creating a perfect angle, and I knew I should throw a counter right hand, a two/three combo, but the fear had me and I took a step back and created space instead. My opponent walked toward me and reset, switching to southpaw, only I didn't see it in time, didn't realize that everything was now reversed, that he was going to throw a straight left and a right hook instead of a straight right and a left hook, and then he'd closed the distance and was in striking range. He threw a straight left that partially landed, and then a right hook, and I saw it coming but I froze and felt it connect, the world suddenly white and flashing, my body involuntarily shutting down. I dropped to one knee and popped back up quickly, and the ref was between us and motioning me to go to the neutral corner for the standing eight count. I tried to gather my wits, to understand what had happened, to wrangle the fear, to banish it, to will it away. I wasn't hurt, and I wasn't tired, but there was a fear in me that felt like it had my whole body submerged in water. Nothing was working like I wanted it to. Not my arms. Not my legs. Not my mind. The ref was talking to me, and over his shoulder I could see my opponent casually waiting for the fight to resume.

"Do you want to continue?"

I heard him ask the question, and I wanted to continue because I didn't want to be as scared as I was, as weak as I was. None of it made any sense. It was just another sparring session, just like Rodney had said, something I had done a hundred times before, and no, maybe I wasn't ten thousand punches good yet, but I was at least five thousand punches good, or eight thousand punches good, and all I needed to do was nod my head and push through the fear and meet that man back in the middle of the ring and do what I had trained to do.

A second or two had passed since the ref had asked if I wanted to continue, but I hadn't answered, and suddenly the ref was waving his hands over his head and the fight was over. "You just need a little more time in the gym," he said. "You'll get there."

I was embarrassed and frustrated, and I felt pathetic, and like I'd let myself down, and like I'd let Rodney down, and even like I'd let Dempsey down, whom I'd wanted more than anything to be able to call later, on the way home, so I could tell him how tough I'd been, how I'd knocked another man out, how I'd excelled at being a man.

But I knew that none of that would happen now because the fight was over and the people in the crowd had begun to get up from their seats. I had lost a fight I felt I was never really in, and it would haunt me for years—not just the loss, but the feeling that I had let myself down, that I had given up, that somewhere deep inside I had wanted to lose because losing was the fastest way out. In the years after that fight, I would punish myself in the gym, in sparring sessions with boxers much better than me, with pros and amateurs, staying in the pocket even when heavy punches landed, accepting every one of them, trying to eradicate whatever it was that had taken over me that day. It would be years before I understood what had happened that day, years before I would recognize that what I felt that day wasn't just fear, but a fundamental lack of trust in myself. I would think of that fight often, in the quiet moments of my life, often when I was lying in bed at night with my eyes closed, replaying every moment, every punch, every counter I didn't throw, every right hand I kept chambered next to my chin. I would see my opponent's face over and over and feel the surprise of his punches, the sting, but I would also begin to see and acknowledge something else, something it would take years for me to accept: that the only way to trust myself was to truly forgive myself—a task I found immeasurably more difficult and scarier than the fight itself.

After my loss in the Gloves, and after I'd tried on a romantic relationship that ultimately didn't stick, I began to feel the gravitational pull from the Midwest with a ferocity I could no longer ignore. I needed to make a change in my life even if it meant that the change would cost me the job I had worked so hard to succeed at.

"Dempsey can't tell you where you have to live," my coworker Steven said when I called him to share how I was feeling. "But he can definitely tell you where you have to live when he's the one sign-ing your paychecks."

I knew Steven was right, but I also knew that it didn't matter anymore. I wanted to be home, in Chicago, where I felt most like myself, building a recovery community and living a sober life in the city I yearned for, not in Charlotte or Baltimore, two cities that had given me experiences that had helped me settle into my sobri-ety, but couldn't replace home. I had reached a point where even if Dempsey fired me after I told him, I was okay with the outcome. I'd just have to figure it out.

When I called to tell him, it went better than expected. "What-ever," he said. "Do what you have to do." I could sense in his voice that he wasn't happy about it, but he wasn't fighting me on the decision anymore, so I got off the phone and began to make plans to move home to Chicago. I had been away for three years, and I was excited to finally be moving back to the place I loved, to the city that had shaped me, to a landscape that felt familiar. But the deci-sion was also fraught, like so many decisions in early sobriety, and there were sacrifices I needed to make in order to get back there. I had managed to find a tenant for the condo I'd bought in Charlotte when I first moved to Baltimore, but it had lost more than half its value when the market crashed. To make matters worse, my tenant called to say that he was leaving when his lease was up if I didn't lower the rent. I had no choice but to capitulate, but the rent, which was never quite enough to cover the mortgage, was now nowhere near covering the mortgage, and the bills were piling up. I kept up with it for as long as I could, but then my tenant moved out any-way, and it seemed like I was throwing good money after bad, and I decided to work with the bank to short sale it, which was really just a nicer name for "foreclosure." My credit score, which had only just begun to climb after I left rehab, was on the decline again, and to complicate the situation even more, the condo I'd bought in Bal-timore was underwater for the same reasons the Charlotte one was.

I decided to put the place up for sale, but the price was too high, and the market was too low, and no one was biting, and I soon realized that there were some things that even sobriety couldn't fix. So not long after listing the place, with one failed investment in Charlotte, and what would later become a second failed investment in Baltimore, I packed everything I owned in a U-Haul truck, turned over the ignition, and started back toward the city I had been trying to get back to since the very day I had left.

IV

SEVEN

When I pulled across the Illinois state line, instead of elation, I felt a sort of dread that I hadn't been expecting. I'd been envisioning the moment I would return home for years—the familiar shape of a bungalow house, the hard vowels of a Chicago accent—but as I crossed over from Indiana to Illinois and made my way toward Oak Lawn, the suburb I'd grown up in, where my mother and stepfather's house was still located, I had the sudden feeling that I was moving backward. My parents were living in Iowa at the time—my stepfather had taken an early retirement from the municipality he'd spent the last twenty years working for and decided to try his hand at dairy farming with his brother-in-law—so they had offered to let me rent their house for six hundred dollars a month. It was a cheaper, better deal than I would find anywhere else, and I was grateful to them for their kindness, but when I pulled into the driveway off Central Avenue and saw the small brick house I'd grown up in, the kitchen windows I'd looked out of as I spooned sugary cereal into my mouth as a boy, the porch I'd sat on smoking Marlboros as a teenager, the spot on the driveway where I'd first called my biological father to ask him why he'd left, it all felt like too much, as if I were reverting to the person I'd been before I'd met Dempsey, before I got sober, before I became the person it now felt like I had always been destined to be.

Later, after I'd unpacked boxes and moved in, during my first train ride into Dempsey's office in the city—the building that had served as the backdrop for getting sober, the place I had arrived at years before, what felt like lifetimes before—I stared out the window of the Metra and watched as the landscape blurred and changed, as we passed loading yards and mechanic shops, junked cars scrapped for parts, semitruck trailers that had graffiti tattooed across their sheet metal. I saw the city in the distance, its skyline elegant and piercing, drawing closer with each minute that passed, and felt that something was happening, something I couldn't quite understand, something that had to do with transformation, with change, with reckoning. It was something I wouldn't understand in that moment, something I couldn't have articulated even if I'd had the language back then, but I would soon learn that what I was feeling that day, which I now know I was also feeling in Baltimore just before I made the decision to return home, was a sort of letting go, a detaching, a decision to slowly loosen the grip I had on the identity I was carrying around. I had been a high-school dropout, a waiter with a GED, a criminal and drug addict consumed by substances that promised a freedom that never came, but with Dempsey's help, with his benevolence, I had transitioned into a sober young businessman, a professional, a person who had once spent so much of his time trying to escape his life, but now wanted nothing more than to be submersed in it, to feel the whole of it—the pain and struggle, the joy, the heartbreak, the realness. What I felt in that moment of letting go was a realization that I would have to move on, to find my own way forward, that I would have to make the decision to leave Dempsey and his company, to break free from the man who had literally saved my life. I would have to take what he had given me and forge a new path— this I knew—but I also knew that it would feel like a betrayal, and perhaps a betrayal was exactly what it was. Dempsey had given me opportunities that had changed the trajectory of my life, gifts that I could never repay, but still I would leave. I would be haunted by one question that even now, two decades after I first met Dempsey,

I'm not sure I know the answer to: To the people who save us, what do we owe?

The office felt different when I returned. It was still on the thirty-fifth floor, and it was still fundamentally the same, but in the time that I'd been gone, a few of my coworkers had moved on to other jobs and their offices had been cleaned out and were now being used for storage. Dempsey's enormous corner office sat unoccupied, no longer existing under a haze of cigar smoke. His belongings were gone—the crystal ashtray, the computer, the football helmet that had been displayed on a shelf behind his desk—and it somehow felt smaller without him in it.

I walked down there one afternoon when there wasn't much going on and passed through the doorway, past the conference table I'd been sitting at when Dempsey had screamed at me to find some humility, and walked to the windows. Down below, miniature men and women shuffled across Wacker Drive, the aerial view of the crosswalk markings made it look like the pedestrians were walking across the rungs of a ladder, and I remembered the first time I'd been in Dempsey's office. It seemed like a lifetime had passed since I'd first sat down in his enormous wingback chair and he'd offered me a job. I turned from the window and looked at the desk he used to sit at and thought of all the afternoons I'd sat across from him while he smoked a cigar, especially those days when he was in a good mood, when the fire-breathing dragon was absent, and remembered how he'd made me feel. In those moments, when he cast his spell and told me about what he was building, about the company, about what *we* were building, about the stock I might receive and the financial future I could have, and all the travel we were going to do and the people we were going to meet, there was nothing—almost nothing—I wouldn't do for him.

As I pondered the scene below me, I thought back to a time maybe a year or so after I'd gotten sober. We were at a meeting at a luxury golf resort in Florida, and Dempsey had arranged a big dinner at a fancy restaurant. It was before Dempsey split with Summer, and she was there with us, sitting to his left, listening to Dempsey tell stories. After dinner had been served and cleared, Summer ordered a cup of coffee, and when it arrived, it was cold. She tried to hide it, but her face gave her away and Dempsey noticed it. I watched from my seat as Dempsey asked her what was wrong. "It's fine, it's fine," she said, but in Dempsey's mind it wasn't fine, and I could see the anger building, the way his jaw set, the way his eyes narrowed. He took the cold cup of coffee and stood up, scanning the restaurant for our waiter, and started walking toward him, quickly. The waiter, who was looking down at a check in his hand, looked up right at the last second, just as Dempsey was closing the distance, just as Dempsey stumbled on purpose and threw the cold coffee all over the waiter's chest. "You gave my wife cold motherfucking coffee, you disrespectful piece of shit," he said, his anger now a full level ten. "Fuck you, you fucking jagoff!" His volume was turned up and nearly everyone in the restaurant was watching what was happening, all the heads at all the tables turned toward him, forks frozen midway between plate and mouth, hands wrapped around water glasses, and then the manager was next to the waiter, and the manager was yelling and the waiter was yelling, and then the cooks in the kitchen had cleared out and they were yelling, and it looked like it was going to be a good old-fashioned brawl. Dempsey was ready for it, and looked like he wanted it, and I knew I needed to be next to him when shit went down, when punches started to fly, so I could back up Dempsey, so I could back up this man who had given me my life back. I stood up quickly and saddled up next to him, fists balled, feet staggered, ready to go, ready to fight, scared of what might happen, of catching charges, of going to jail again, of blowing up everything I'd worked so hard for. But this man had saved me and I wouldn't have any of it if it weren't for him, and I knew that I owed him. I owed him for everything I had, for sobriety, for the debt he'd help me pay off, for the trips to Colorado to see my daughter, for the five thousand dollars he'd once given me to pay the full balance of the back child support I owed. There was no choice in the moment, not really. I had to throw punches with him, to stand my ground next to him, to accept whatever fate might come.

The argument spilled out the door and into the amber glow and sticky air of the warm Florida night—and then suddenly it was over and we were storming away, the check left unpaid, the whole restaurant a sea of wide eyes and open mouths. We reassembled at an outdoor table near another part of the resort, me and Dempsey and Steven and a few other people, my heart still pumping, my hands still shaking, and Dempsey lit a cigar and laughed. I watched as he took a long pull, the cherry glowing orange in the dark, and behind him I could see through a set of double doors into the lobby of the hotel. Dempsey laughed and laughed about the look on the waiter's face, about the stain on his shirt, about the cooks who'd cleared the kitchen, about how close we'd come to being in a scene from an old western where the saloon erupts into a huge fight and the whole place gets trashed. But just then, as he blew a cloud of smoke above his head, I saw three police officers walk through the front door of the resort. Dempsey's back was to the door, and he couldn't see them, but I knew what they were there for, knew that no one starts a fight in a resort restaurant and gets away with it. "The cops just walked in," I said to Dempsey, leaning forward on the table. "You better get the fuck out of here." His expression changed and he grabbed the arm of his chair and used it to help twist himself around so he could see them, and I watched as a hotel employee pointed in our direction, and the three officers started for us. Dempsey looked back at me and smiled then shook his head. "Fuck," he said. "I guess I need to deal with this." Then he rose and met the officers, who walked him over to a spot near the tiled border of the pool, where the light shimmered off the water, and began questioning him. I watched him for a moment, then looked around at where we were, at this extravagant resort in Florida, the nicest place I'd ever been, and at the palm trees lit by spotlights, and I noticed how the air smelled of the ocean, like salt and seaweed, and how over in the corner, the man who had given me all of it, this life, this sobriety, this opportunity at something so much better and different from anything I could have ever imagined, was being questioned by the police for nearly starting a fistfight in the crowded dining room of an upscale restaurant. None of it made any sense, and maybe none of it ever would, and the thing I would think about years later, when it was all a distant memory, was that maybe none of it actually had to. Because maybe the fact that it had all happened in the first place was enough.

A few weeks later, I stared at the computer screen in my office and read the PDF containing the specifics of the job offer over again, focusing on two lines that appeared in the third paragraph. "Your offer is also contingent on the completion of an undergraduate degree. In a separate document, we will outline the details of providing you full tuition at an approved local university and the time frame to complete the degree."

It was June of 2009 and I'd been home for a few months, settling into the routine that I'd missed so much when I was gone. I took the Metra train from a station just a few blocks from my parents' home in Oak Lawn into the city each day, hitting the gym after work then riding the train back to the suburbs, where I'd make dinner in the small house I'd grown up in, listening to traffic pass on Central Avenue, hearing the familiar sound of the warning bells before the train lumbered by, sometimes finding an AA meeting to head to in the evenings.

I'd begun seriously thinking about finding a new job when I'd been approached by a man who worked for a competitor of Dempsey's.

We'd gotten to know each other a bit during conferences we'd both attended, and he worked for a large company based in a suburb of Detroit. "You should come into the office and see what it's like," he said, as we chatted in a hotel hallway after a conference session one day. "It's a little over an hour flight from Chicago. What do you have to lose?"

I took a couple of days off work and made the short trip from Chicago to Detroit, and then I rented a car and drove thirty minutes to the company's headquarters, a sprawling building situated just off the highway in a Detroit suburb dotted with historic Victorian homes. The building had a fitness center and a cafeteria and hundreds of employees and a sea of cubicles and dozens of nice offices, and it was more buttoned up than Dempsey's company, more conservative, more professional. The organization was publicly traded and published salary levels and compensation tiers, and it had a bonus structure and an employee development program. It felt to me like it was a long way from Dempsey's company, certainly in the early years when he had first hired me, but even now, after the acquisition by the company in Charlotte, which had grown the head count by fifty or sixty employees overnight.

I met with the man who had first approached me, and our meeting went well, and afterward, once I was back in Chicago, I couldn't stop thinking about what the opportunity might mean for me. It was a chance to learn and grow professionally in a real way, a way that I simply couldn't at Dempsey's company even though I was now a vice president, a way that would allow me to shore up the career knowledge I was short on, to carve out a career path that felt more stable, and more predictable. But I also knew that it would feel unforgivable to Dempsey, and that a decision to leave and go to a competitor—no matter what the offer was, no matter what the opportunity was, no matter how I tried to explain it—would feel to him like a declaration of war.

When the offer letter came and I read it for the first time, when I read the words that explained that I would need to complete my undergraduate degree as a requirement for my employment, but that the company would pay for it, words that must have seemed unremarkable and boilerplate to the person who wrote them, words they must have included in dozens of other offer letters, my eyes welled up and my vision narrowed and a whole future that I had never considered suddenly became visible. Though I had been scared to even articulate it, I'd wanted to attend college ever since I'd gotten sober, but it just never seemed possible. It was too much money and it was too impractical and it wasn't important to Dempsey, which meant that it couldn't be important to me. Except that, reading the letter that day, I knew that it was, and that it had been since the day I'd left rehab, maybe longer. Because even though I'd gotten sober and become a professional in some sense of the word, even though I now owned dress shoes and slacks and no longer smelled like fryer grease at the end of the work day, I still felt deeply inadequate. I still felt like an impostor. I was thirty-one years old with a GED, and I wanted to attend college more than I ever had before, to walk a tree-lined campus somewhere in the city as a newly enrolled student, to share space with other students, to listen to a lecture by a real professor. I wanted to prove to myself that I was more—more than a kid who couldn't make it through one biology class without being thrown out, more than a kid who couldn't finish high school, more than a kid with a felony and a criminal record.

As I sat in my office that day on the thirty-fifth floor of the building I had come to for the first time six years before, envisioning a future that was suddenly possible, I knew that I would take the job. It wasn't about the pay or the benefits or the people or the work, or maybe it was—but it was more about the education—or, perhaps more accurately, what the education would mean for me. And yet, even as I sat there, certain of my decision, knowing that my time with Dempsey was coming to an end, I knew that there would be a price to pay. Dempsey had always said that I didn't owe him anything, that he was only doing "the next right thing," but in the weeks and months after accepting the offer, I would learn that what he said and what he did were different, and the price I would pay, the balance I owed, was quickly coming due.

EIGHT

"You know that if I do this," I said into the phone, leaning back in my desk chair at home, the offer letter pulled up on the computer screen in front of me, "that Dempsey's going to sue me, right?"

I was talking to the man who'd offered me the job, trying to get him to understand that I wasn't being alarmist, but practical. He'd had his own dealings with Dempsey over the last year or two, and he'd gotten a taste of the fire-breathing dragon on a couple of occasions. Nevertheless, I got the impression that he thought it would all blow over, that I was being dramatic.

"Yeah, maybe," he said, "but come on. You're not a hostage. You can leave whenever you want to—and this is a great opportunity. Imagine where you'll be in a couple of years."

I grabbed the mouse and scrolled down to the part of the letter where it talked about the degree. I highlighted the sentence with the cursor and stared at the words. I'd already spent hours on the internet looking into all the undergraduate programs in Chicago, reading about the University of Chicago and Northwestern University and UIC. Each school looked more incredible than the one before it, but it was DePaul University's program that I'd spent the most time thinking about. They had a campus in the Loop, close to all the train stations, and it was exactly what I wanted—a school in the city I loved, with a name that carried weight.

"Look," I said, "I think it's the right move for me, and I want to do it, but if I do get sued, you guys absolutely need to cover the defense. I know you think I'm overreacting, but it's the only way I'll take the offer. If I get sued, you guys need to ante up. I literally don't have the money to defend myself in a lawsuit."

The man on the other end of the phone sounded distracted, like he was reading an email while trying to have a conversation. "What? Yeah, okay. It's fine. I'll set up a meeting with you and our chief legal counsel, and you guys can figure out the specifics. But I'm sure it'll be fine, Tim. Just try to relax. This is a good thing, for you—and for us."

When I hung up the phone, I wasn't convinced. How much would a lawsuit cost in the end? Fifty grand? A hundred? I had a feeling that things were about to blow up, but I knew there was no turning back. I was going to take the job. To me, it would feel like progress. To Dempsey, it would feel like treason.

I wrote the fourth draft of my resignation letter just before I took a few days off to meet my family at a house we'd all rented in Gun Lake, Michigan, a three-and-a-half-hour drive from Chicago. It was a place we'd visited in the summers when I was a child. My stepfather's entire family—he had a brother and six sisters—would meet and rent cabins in a lakeside community called Whispering Pines, and we'd spend a week fishing for bass and northern pike in the early mornings, playing board games in the afternoons while the sun dropped low over the lake, and roasting marshmallows for s'mores over an open fire in the evenings, as lightning bugs flickered on and off in the inky black. We'd recently revamped the tradition, though it was just my immediate family now, and I'd decided to send my resignation letter to Dempsey from the safety of a cabin hundreds of miles away from him. I was certain that I was making the right choice for myself, but I was incredibly uncertain about how it would ultimately play out. I emailed my resignation to him at the end of the day on a Friday, while my stepfather grilled hamburgers outside on the lawn, blue-gray smoke swirling toward the swaying branches of the big oak tree that sprung from the ground next to the cabin, knowing Dempsey would view it as a coward's move, which in some sense it was. For years I would wonder if I should have found the courage to fly to Charlotte to tell him in person. But I was scared of Dempsey's reaction, or maybe anxious is a better word for it, or maybe it's more accurate to say that I simply didn't want to deal with it at all, either in person or over the phone. It was as if the moment I knew for certain that I was leaving I could no longer fathom enduring even one more second of his anger.

I had agonized over every word of my resignation letter, typing and retyping draft after draft, trying to convey how grateful I was to Dempsey for all he had done for me, thanking him over and over, trying to find language that would express exactly how much I understood my life had changed because of him. I wanted him to know, to really know, that I knew, that I really knew, how significantly he had changed my life. I wanted him to see that this was how it had to be, that I couldn't be there forever, that if I was to grow and learn and progress in both my life and my career, that I would have to move on. It was magical thinking, of course, and selfish, I know now. But it also felt like it was all I could do. I had to move forward, and I couldn't do that with him. At least, not anymore.

Within minutes of hitting send, I had a response that was exactly as I had thought. I was a prideful, selfish prick "who lived in his mommy and daddy's house," and I better get ready because "this shit's not over" and there would be hell to pay.

Within hours of receiving his response, my company cell phone was shut off. I spent the night at the lakeside cabin, tossing and turning in my bed, and by morning I was panicky. I said a hasty goodbye to my family, feeling like I needed to be back in Chicago, even though I knew there was nothing I could do, and I drove the three and a half hours home with a multitude of worst-case scenarios playing out in my head. I slept terribly that night, and again the night after, and then Monday morning there was a knock on my front door. I didn't recognize the woman standing there. I opened the door. "Timothy Hillegonds?" she said. "Yes," I said. "You've been served," she said, and handed me an inches-thick stack of papers.

After reading through the first few paragraphs, I became aware that Dempsey was suing me for a litany of things, most of which I'd never even heard of: Tortious Interference with Existing Contracts and Business Relations, Violation of the Illinois Trade Secrets Act, Breach of Fiduciary Responsibility, Breach of Contract, Conversion, Conspiracy, and Unjust Enrichment. I sat on the couch with my face flushed and heart beating, stressed beyond description, and flipped through the pages of the lawsuit in my parents' living room, the same room I'd watched cartoons in as a kid, the same room where we'd opened presents on Christmas morning, the same room I'd practiced my piano lessons in as a child.

When I called my new employer to let him know what had happened, he did his best to assuage my fears, to tell me that it would all be all right, but in the living room of the house I'd grown up in, which now felt both foreign and familiar, I couldn't keep the sinking feeling at bay. I felt like what had happened was incredibly unfair, like the lawsuit was frivolous and cruel, but I also felt like it was exactly what I deserved. It was suddenly clear to me that this was the price I would pay for my recovery. This was the balance due.

It was almost a relief to finally know the cost.

A day later, there was another knock at the door, and this time it was a man standing on the concrete steps of my childhood home. I took a deep breath and opened the door partway. "You Tim?" he said. "Yeah," I said. "I'm an investigator hired by your former employer. I'm here to collect all your company property. It's my understanding that you have a computer and a few other things that belong to them. Can I come in?"

He was right that I still had my computer, but I hadn't yet been able to figure out what files I needed to take with me. It was lying on the desk in the living room, which was directly behind me, but I was fairly certain he couldn't see it due to the way that I was standing.

"No, you can't come in," I said, "but I'll come out there." I slipped through the door and pulled it shut behind me. I wasn't sure what to say, so I opted to say nothing and waited for him to speak.

He told me that he had instructions to retrieve the computer and any paper files that I had. I told him I didn't have anything at the moment, not the computer, not the files, nor anything else. He raised his eyebrows and it was clear that he didn't believe me, and he was right not to, but there was no way I was letting him in the house to look, and no way that I was giving up my computer until I had a chance to think about what, if anything, I needed from it. I had years of personal files on there—writing, contacts, legal documents from my various real estate failures, pictures—and I hadn't been able to transfer any of it off the computer yet. So I gave him some bullshit answer, and he told me he'd be back the next day, and then I watched as he walked back to his car, gave me one last glance as he got in, and drove away.

As soon as he was gone, I grabbed my car keys. I needed a hard drive to transfer the files onto, and it felt like the sooner I did it the better. There was a Best Buy a few miles away, so I started my car and backed out of the driveway, heart pounding, mouth dry, feeling like the main operative in a spy movie. I went one direction then doubled back and went the other, circling the block, obsessively glancing in the rearview mirror, convinced the investigator was following me, aware of how ridiculous I was being, but also sure that I had every reason to be paranoid. I knew I hadn't done anything wrong, and that switching jobs was a perfectly acceptable decision that people made every day, but it didn't change the fact that being sued, being served with papers at the house I lived in, felt threatening in a way that I hadn't felt since the last time I'd been arrested, the year before I'd started working for Dempsey.

It was not long after I'd moved back from Colorado, after I'd left the state in a hurry, leaving more than one active warrant in my wake. They were misdemeanor warrants, though, which meant they were non-extraditable, but they would still show up every time a police officer ran a background check over the radio. That night, I'd been walking on Chicago's lakefront path with a girl I had been on a few dates with, casually drinking wine out of a red Solo cup, and a police officer had approached me, asking me what was in it. I told him it was wine, convinced I had nothing to hide, and he made me pour it out, saying there was a no-open-container policy on the lakefront. It seemed like that would be the end of it. But then he said that he still needed to run my name. So I gave him my ID, and he walked a few feet away from me, speaking into the radio on his shoulder. I watched as his demeanor suddenly shifted. He walked back over to me and said that I had warrants in another state. I said that I knew, but that they were misdemeanor warrants in Colorado, so why should he care? He said that maybe that was indeed the case, but he couldn't be sure because there was some sort of problem with the computer system and they'd need to sort it out at the station.

"Wait, what?" I said, confused and incredulous, and then my hands were behind my back, and the handcuffs were clicking tighter and tighter, and I was looking out at the lake, where the lights from the lampposts sparkled off the water, the girl I was with standing off to the side looking concerned, waiting for some sort of explanation from me, some sort of clue that this was all a misunderstanding.

But it wasn't, and the next thing I knew I was being put in the back of a paddy wagon and taken to a Chicago police station, where I'd have to wait to have it all sorted out. I was so tired of being arrested, so tired of having my freedom taken away, so tired of trying to change but then feeling like I hadn't changed at all.

As I sat in the back of that windowless police vehicle, alone and bouncing around, what I didn't yet fully understand was that in order to make a true, lasting transformation in my life, I would need to face all of it. I couldn't simply move locations and expect that to be the end of it. I needed to come to terms with everything I'd done and the person that I'd been in Colorado. Because if I didn't, the only thing that had really changed was my geography. And if I had learned anything from my move from Chicago to Colorado, and then from Colorado back to Chicago, it was that changing your geography and changing yourself were two entirely different tasks.

True to their word my new employer hired an attorney for me, and I met him at his office in the western suburbs of Chicago. He was tall and thin with glasses that sat toward the end of a prominent nose, a full head of hair parted neatly to one side, and he seemed to have a vast understanding of the case against me by the time we met.

"Look," he said, flipping the page on the complaint in front of him, "they're grasping at straws with most of this stuff. You never signed a non-compete, so you're well within your rights to go to a competitor. I mean, clearly, this is emotional. But here's the thing. They're going to tie you up with proceedings for a long while. It's just the way it works. They know they don't have a real shot at winning a case against you, especially one that would award them damages, which means the only real point of this whole charade is to make your life hell." He paused and leaned back in his chair, straightening his tie so it rested neatly atop the buttons of his white Oxford shirt. "They've got money to spend, and there are all sorts of corporate tricks they can use to jam us up—injunctions, temporary restraining orders, continuances—the list goes on and on."

I sat in a small wooden chair in front of his desk, which was nice enough, but it was nothing like Dempsey's, nothing like the expensive red leather chair I'd spent so much time in, looking up at him, hanging on his every word while he smoked his cigar, listening to him plot and scheme about getting an edge over someone here, an advantage over someone there. I looked across my attorney's office at a small bookshelf containing volumes of thick legal books, all neatly lined up in order. On the top shelf was a picture of his family, and what looked like some sort of business award. I recognized the name of the company who had issued it, a company that had handled some of our clients' financial claims. At one point, Dempsey had become obsessed with handling these claims in-house, which was something he couldn't do at the time and had to outsource, and he was convinced that it would give him the competitive advantage he needed to corner even more of the market.

"Here's what I want you to do," Dempsey said to me late one afternoon, as I rode with him down the elevator from the thirty-fifth floor. "I know the idiot that runs the place over there, so I'm going to get you an interview. I want you to go to work for them. Not forever, and not for good, but long enough to learn how they do everything they do. Memorize all their ideas and techniques. Read all their material. Figure out their software. Learn all their shit. And then once you know it all, quit and come back here with all the intel."

I stared at him with what must have been a stunned look on my face, thinking that it sounded like one of the worst ideas I'd ever heard in my life. "You want me to go to *work* for them?" I said, while gravity pulled us toward the lobby. "Yeah," he said. "Think about it. You learn how they do what they do, and then you come back here and we use what you know to gain the advantage and bring the claims in-house. We'll be fucking unstoppable. And they'll never see it coming."

The elevator reached the ground floor with a ding, and we stepped out onto the large-format polished-marble tiles, Dempsey's wooden heels clicking against them as we walked. I had absolutely no desire to go work for another company, absolutely no desire to get used to a new routine. But I also knew it wasn't a negotiation. Dempsey had a plan and I could see there was no use fighting it. "Fine, fuck it," I said as we stopped near the revolving door of the lobby. "Set it up and we'll make it happen."

Two weeks later I sat for an interview at their office in the West Loop, in a rehabilitated loft building with high ceilings and exposed timber beams. They had me take a personality test and asked me about the work I did for Dempsey—easy questions that I knew the answers to—and it was clear it was more of a formality than anything else. When it came time to talk about my salary, I sensed an opportunity. If I was going to uproot everything, I wanted to be paid for it—and paid as much as possible.

Seated across from me at a conference room table, my interviewer asked about compensation. I was making $62,500 at Dempsey's company, which was so much more than I'd ever made waiting tables that I still sometimes wondered how all of it had even happened. It felt like it was just yesterday that I was fetching extra sides of honey-mustard dressing.

"I need eighty thousand to make it work," I said, feeling about as confident as I'd ever felt in my life, since I had no desire whatsoever to actually work there. I was also unwilling to negotiate. Part of me was searching for an excuse to blow the whole thing up so I wouldn't have to go through with it. Maybe we wouldn't be able to come to terms, and everything could just go back to normal.

The man on the other side of the table agreed to my figure so quickly that I instantly realized I'd left money on the table. Even though I felt like I'd made real progress in becoming a serious businessperson, it was clear that I still had so much to learn—about negotiation, yes, but also about power and leverage and courage. Regardless, I left the office feeling better than when I'd arrived, wondering if maybe it would all work out in the end. At the very least, I'd learn more about the business of finance, which I felt I knew strikingly little about. Dempsey wasn't big on details, and I always felt when it came to the specifics, I knew about half as much as I should.

Later that day, I met Dempsey at the cigar shop he loved off LaSalle Street, not far from the Board of Trade, where I'd had that interview with Summer's company years before, when I was still a waiter. We sat opposite each other on leather chesterfield sofas, the air thick with tobacco smoke, a coffee table with two large crystal ashtrays between us. Dempsey had a steel cigar cutter in his hand and was just about to slice off the end of his Padron. He leaned forward so the ashtray would catch it.

"How'd it go?" he said, as the blade quickly did its work.

"Good," I said. A bus on LaSalle Street let off its brakes and moved past the store, unblocking the sunlight it had been holding back, which quickly cut through the smoke like a guillotine. Outside the store's window, a steady stream of people filed by, their shadows dancing on the floor by our feet. "I got the feeling that it's a done deal," I said. "I think I'm just waiting on the paperwork and a start date at this point."

Dempsey took a long draw from his cigar, leaned back, and blew the smoke high into the air above him, where a vent in the ceiling pulled it through its louvers. He turned the cigar sideways and blew on the cherry, watched as it glowed, the dried tobacco leaves crackling softly. "I've been thinking," he said, contemplating his cigar. "I think we should pull the plug on this thing. We can figure out how they do what they do some other way."

I leaned forward. "Yeah?" I said.

"Yeah." He took another draw.

The relief I felt was immediate, but it was followed by another feeling: financial panic. I'd already done the math to figure out how much my new paycheck would be. I had negotiated an almost-eighteen-thousand-dollar raise. And even though it was essentially a thought experiment at that point, I was already spending the money in my mind, and I didn't want to give up the increase in income.

"I mean, you'll get no argument from me," I said, sitting up a little bit straighter. "But there's this one thing."

"What?" he said.

"I negotiated a higher salary."

"So?" he said.

"So you need to match it."

My heart was flogging my rib cage, but I could sense that this was the play. I needed to stand my ground and not blink first. Which was almost impossible to do because I knew that at any moment, the fire-breathing dragon might show up and torch everything, the surrounding public be damned.

Dempsey didn't say anything at first, just looked at me while I did my best to hold my ground without giving away how nervous I was. He sat up and scooched forward, reached over and ashed his cigar. We were eye to eye. "You motherfucker," he said slowly and quietly, a small, almost imperceptible smile appearing on his face.

I smirked, the tension I felt releasing, relieved that the dragon had stayed in its den. "What can I say?" I said, leaning back against the sofa. "I learned from the best."

He shook his head and laughed. "Not bad, Hillegonds," he said. "Not bad. It's about time you fucking learned something."

Not long after my initial meeting with my attorney, he called to tell me that Dempsey had filed for, and been granted, a temporary restraining order, which my attorney explained to me was common in civil cases like mine. "It's different from what you're probably familiar with in domestic cases," he said to me while I held my cell phone to my ear, weaving through people pulling Rollaboard suitcases at Midway Airport, on my way to catch a flight to Detroit. "What a TRO does is limit what you can do—who you can contact, what activities you can engage in—until a comprehensive hearing can be held where the court makes a formal decision."

I walked onto the moving walkway and pulled off to the side, stopping so I could focus on the conversation. "What does that mean in practical terms? What can't I do?"

A mom with two kids in tow filed past me, and I flashed her a quick smile, mouthing the word "sorry" as she squeezed by me pulling a bedazzled pink suitcase.

"It means you can't talk to anyone you talked to while you were with Dempsey's company. At least for the time being."

"What? I don't get it," I said, frustrated, since the entirety of my new job was predicated on being able to cultivate the relationships I'd built over the years. "I never signed a non-compete. I'm not breaking any laws. How can they do this?"

On the other end of the phone, I heard the distinct sound of papers rustling and a woman's voice in the background. I figured it was his legal secretary. I heard him say a muffled "thanks," and then he was talking to me again. "Look, I know this is frustrating, but it's part of it. Remember what I told you when we met? This isn't about you doing anything wrong. It's about making you pay. And one of the ways they're going to try and make you pay is by making it as difficult as possible to do your job. We'll fight it, of course, but it's going to take time. It's a process." He paused. "Which reminds me, they want to depose you soon. I need to give them some dates. Are you familiar with what a deposition is?"

I was. A couple of years before, I'd been deposed as part of a claim that had gone into litigation. During the prep session I'd been required to attend with our attorney, he'd had me sit in a chair in his office while he paced in front of me. "The most important thing to remember," he'd said as I looked up at him, feeling as if I were about to take an exam I hadn't studied for, "is that you need to answer each question truthfully, while giving away as little information as possible." He'd abruptly stopped pacing then looked right at me. "Do you know what time it is?" I'd glanced at the clock on his desk, convinced there was no way I could give away too much information by answering such a simple question. "It's 1:47," I'd said. "Wrong," he'd said. "I didn't ask you what time it was. I asked you *if you knew* what time it was. It's a yes or no question, Tim. You need to listen carefully and pay more attention."

I reached the end of the moving walkway in B Terminal and stepped off, quickly pulling my suitcase over the transition strip. "Yeah, I'm familiar," I said.

"Okay, good. Then we'll get it set up. I'll prep you beforehand, but I need to warn you, Tim. I get the feeling they're going to try and dig up some dirt on you and try to use it to attack your character."

"What does that mean?"

"You've got a pretty colorful past, yeah?"

"What does that have to do with anything?"

"Well, technically nothing. But I imagine they're going to try to use it against you in one way or another."

I let out an audible sigh and fell into a chair near my gate. It felt like no matter what I did, my past was always with me, ready to be weaponized. "Whatever," I said. "I dealt with all of that. Paid my debts. Mended my relationships. Besides, it was a long time ago, and I'm not that guy anymore."

"I know, Tim. But my job as your attorney is to make sure you're ready for whatever it is they throw at you. I've been doing this for a while, and my instincts tell me that this will probably get ugly. It's nothing we can't deal with, but we're going to need to work together closely on this. You tell me everything. I'll give you some strategies. And then we'll get through it together one question at a time. You just need to remain calm and measured. That's the main thing. If you can do that, we'll get through it no problem."

The gate agent came over the loudspeaker and announced that my flight was boarding.

"Fine. Whatever. I'm sure it'll all work out."

"All right then, I'll be in touch soon."

I hit the button to end the call and put the phone in my pocket, wanting nothing more than to get on a plane that would take me to someone else's life.

My deposition took place on enemy turf—at Dempsey's attorney's office. It was in a glass conference room in a new glass and steel high-rise with an incredible view of Lake Michigan, a few blocks away from where Dempsey's office had been located. When I arrived, my attorney was already there. He met me in the lobby.

"Remember," he said, "we've got nothing to hide. Just stick to the script we practiced. Answer their questions and stay calm. If you don't know the answer, though, don't guess. Say you can't recall. Got it?"

The elevator opened and a woman in a pantsuit carrying an expensive-looking bag got off, glanced at us, and walked toward the conference room.

I waited until she was out of earshot. "Yeah, I got it," I said.

A few days earlier I'd driven out to his office, and we'd done some prep for the deposition. I felt ready to go, but I was also nervous—and agitated. I was having a hard time dealing with the fact that I couldn't simply leave my job like a normal person. Instead, here I was, months after giving my resignation, feeling more like a criminal than a guy trying to better his life.

My attorney glanced over at the glass-walled conference room. Dempsey's two attorneys, both impeccably dressed in dark-blue suits, were inside chatting with one another. They glanced at us and nodded.

"All right," my attorney said, "we need to get in there. The sooner we get started, the sooner you can get out of here."

A few minutes later, after all the pleasantries had been dispensed, I sat across from Dempsey's lead attorney. He had a legal pad in front of him, and he was peering down at it from behind a pair of stylish dark frames. My attorney, who was seated next to me, told him we were ready to proceed.

The first few questions were softballs—my full name, how long I'd worked for Dempsey, what my various titles had been over the years. I answered them slowly and tried to relax, but I was on edge, and the longer it went on, the more frustration I felt, and the more anger I felt toward the attorney in front of me. I knew myself well enough to know that I needed to watch myself, to focus on staying calm, to not get worked up, because even though it was Dempsey who was known for the fire-breathing dragon, there was also one inside me, one that I'd been working hard to eradicate from my life. It was that anger that had gotten me in so much trouble when I was young, anger that had fueled the fights and arrests that had lengthened my criminal record, that had preceded the time I spent in jail, that had fueled so much of the drinking and using I had done in my youth. It had been years since I'd given in to it in any real way, but I could feel my annoyance mounting, and I knew I needed to be careful.

The examining attorney glanced at his file then looked up at me. "So, you lived in Colorado, Tim? And you have a daughter?"

My anger was instant and intense. "What the fuck does that have to do with anything?"

"Tim," my attorney said. He put his hand on my forearm briefly, his gold watch peeking out from underneath his shirt cuff.

"It's just a question, Tim," the opposing attorney said. "I'm establishing a few facts here." He looked at me with what seemed like a smirk, and I wanted to reach across the space between us, grab his tie, and bounce his head off the lacquered table. "You lived in

Colorado and you have a daughter, and—" He paused, put his file down, and looked directly at me. "And you got yourself in quite a bit of trouble there, didn't you? Quite a few misdemeanors, and, it says here, a felony for trying to outrun the police in a vehicle?"

I looked at my attorney, but he said nothing, so I turned back toward Dempsey's attorney, trying to keep my voice at a reasonable volume. "I thought we were here to talk about my work for Dempsey, not some shit that happened a million years ago, and certainly not about my daughter. I'll tell you right now we're not talking about my daughter, so you can keep her the fuck out of this. And my past is old news."

"In case you're unaware, you're not the one deciding what we do and don't talk about."

"That's funny. Because it seems like that's exactly what I'm doing."

"You do understand that if you refuse to answer my questions, your refusal will be noted in the record, which the judge will read, right?"

"Tim," my attorney interjected, "please just answer the question."

I ignored him. "We can do this all day, but I'm telling you it's a waste of time. You want to ask me about my time with Dempsey, fine. You want to ask me about my work, fine. Ask away. But this shit about my past and my daughter is a non-fucking-starter."

"Let's take a break," my attorney said.

"You need to get your client in order, counsel. If this keeps up, then I'll have no choice but to suspend the deposition for unprofessional conduct and ask for judicial intervention."

"Just give me a minute to talk to my client."

He stood, and I did too, following him through the door and out into the lobby. We walked back toward the spot near the elevators where we'd been talking earlier. "Look," he said, stopping. "You can't do what you just did. You can't swear and refuse to answer the questions he's asking you. You just can't. It might feel unfair to you, and you might be frustrated, but it doesn't matter because they're allowed to ask you about your daughter and your past. And by getting angry and flustered, you're feeding right into their strategy. When the judge reads through the deposition, he's just reading words. There's no context whatsoever. There's no nuance. It's just going to record that the examining attorney asked you a reasonable question and that you gave an unreasonable response. And how do you think that's going to affect our case? How do you think that's going to influence how the judge thinks about the accusations against you? I've been doing this long enough to tell you exactly what's going to happen. He's going to start to think that maybe you're not as innocent as you say you are. Maybe you're not the little guy getting pummeled by the big mean corporation and their big mean emotional leader, which is what we're basically saying." He paused and took a deep breath then let it out slowly. "You need to get a hold of yourself, Tim. If you want to help yourself, you'll calm down, answer his questions, and do it like a professional adult. I'm not saying you have to like it, but this is where we're at. This is what's happening."

I knew he was right. I put both of my palms up to my face and rubbed it then used my fingers to push hard against my eyeballs, watching the kaleidoscope behind my closed eyes expand and contract. When I opened them, I waited for the picture in front of me to float back together. When it did, I spoke in a voice much calmer than the one I'd used in the conference room.

"I know you're right, but that guy's such a fucking prick. I can barely keep myself from reaching across the table and slapping him."

"I get it, but it doesn't change anything. You need to pull yourself together. Can you do that?"

"Let's just get this over with."

When the deposition resumed, it was more or less the same line of questioning, aimed at painting a portrait of me as a deadbeat father and criminal who was not to be trusted, but I managed to make it through the rest of the session with minimal swearing, and only one more break, which I managed to initiate before completely losing my cool.

Afterward, I stood outside on the sidewalk with my attorney, people streaming past us, a doorman blowing a whistle every few seconds, trying to flag a taxi for a man in a khaki trench coat.

"I'm not going to sugarcoat it, Tim," my attorney said, switching his briefcase to his other hand to avoid hitting a runner in a neon tank top trying to squeeze past us. "That wasn't great. It's not the worst deposition I've ever been in, but it's up there. You certainly didn't help our case, though. That much we know."

I looked across the street, where a man stood watching his dog, which was stretched out on the end of its leash, its hind leg raised while it doused the corner of a *Chicago Tribune* newspaper machine.

"I know," I said, as the dog trotted away with its owner. "And I'm sorry I lost my cool."

My adrenaline and anger had mostly worn off, and now I just felt ashamed and defeated. It was all starting to take a toll on me—the stress of the lawsuit, the fact that I couldn't do my new job the way I wanted to because of the TRO, the constant feelings of frustration and rage because it all just seemed so ridiculously unfair.

My attorney glanced over as a man walking his bike maneuvered past us. "We've got to hope the judge's reaction isn't as bad as what we think it might be, but it's not the end of the world. Just hang in there and keep yourself out of trouble. Don't talk to anyone that you're not supposed to. I mean that too—no one. We can't give them any reason to jam us up any more than they already have."

I nodded and looked back across the street. The man with the dog was gone, but another one was sniffing around the newspaper machine, getting ready to mark it.

"I'll keep my nose clean," I said.

"Good, now get yourself home and I'll follow up with you soon."

With that, he walked over to the doorman and asked him to flag a cab. The doorman nodded and blew his whistle. A few seconds later, a cab pulled up. My attorney got inside, nodded at me one last time, and was gone.

NINE

The lawsuit proceeded the way most lawsuits do: slowly and methodically and expensively. My new employer and I were determined to make the best of it, so my job description was modified and my duties were changed and I did what I could to be useful and productive in ways that didn't violate my TRO. For the first few months, I flew to Detroit on Tuesdays and back home to Chicago on Fridays, doing what I could to assimilate into the new job and the new culture, but what neither I nor my employer was willing to admit, at least not in that first year, was that nothing was working out the way we had hoped.

Nevertheless, I chose to focus on what I could, which turned out to be school, and I dove into it with the enthusiasm of someone who'd just won the lottery. After filling out the application and writing the dean a letter that explained the felony charge on my record, I'd been accepted into, and had enrolled in, a bachelor's program at DePaul University. As I walked into the eleven-story building at 1 East Jackson Boulevard that first day—one of the four or five buildings that made up the Loop campus—I looked up at a DePaul banner posted high above the street. "Big plans. Bold dreams," it read. *Damn right*, I thought and snapped a picture with my iPhone.

The classes I took at DePaul were held in the evenings, and I'd worked out a deal with my new employer that meant I could be home on Mondays to accommodate my class schedule. On those evenings, as the sky darkened over the city and the skyscraper lights glowed to life, as taxis and cars and buses and bikes whizzed by on

State Street, I would order a small cup of coffee from the Barnes and Noble café on the first floor of the building and sip it as I rode up the elevator to my classroom, excited for what I was about to learn, feeling as if I was finally becoming the person I was always meant to be. I was taking classes in business and in writing, and through the books I was reading and the people I was meeting, my world had suddenly opened up in a way that was different from, but just as transformative as, it had with Dempsey. I think it's fair to say that I knew within the first few minutes of my first class at DePaul that I wanted to finish my undergraduate degree and continue my education, that I wanted to get a master's degree, that I wanted to study business and art and writing in a real and serious way, because I loved the work and I loved what I was learning, but also because I loved the way it made me feel about myself. I had lived for so long with an image of myself as a high-school dropout with a drug and alcohol problem, as a rebel and a screw-up, as a person who was nice enough to be around, and sometimes entertaining and funny, but certainly not a person to be taken seriously, and certainly not an academic or an intellectual. But on those nights when I sat at a small desk in a small classroom in a historic building in downtown Chicago, in the city that I'd loved like a romantic partner for as long as I could remember, I felt worthy—of the changes I'd made, of sobriety, of the life I felt so lucky to be living. On the nights that I sat in that classroom high above the city streets, I felt that I finally accepted myself for who I was—a wayward son who had gotten lost out there in the world and had finally made it home.

It was a turn of events that I never saw coming. I first heard about it at work—Dempsey had unexpectedly and suddenly resigned from the company he had founded and then sold. The details came to me in fragments from people I worked with who had heard it from their contacts. Evidently, in an effort that seemed both punitive and strategic, Dempsey had tried to stage a maneuver where he would take employees in key roles with him to the new organization he was assuming an executive position at, thereby temporarily crippling his old company. But a few of the folks who were supposed to go with him had second thoughts at the last minute and ended up staying, and his plan failed, and Dempsey ended up with the exact same thing that I had—a new job and a lawsuit.

It was completely absurd to think that the man who'd hired me and fired me and rehired me and then sued me was now being sued by the exact same company for the exact same thing as me—quitting and going to a competitor organization. It seemed as if it was karma. Or, at the very least, a form of poetic justice—and I'd be lying if I said that it didn't bring me a smidge of satisfaction. The universe, it seemed, was balancing itself.

At first, I thought Dempsey's departure would mean the lawsuit against me would be dropped. After all, with Dempsey no longer in the picture, what was the point? It had always been his anger that had fueled the case, not any real concern over my ability to take business from him, so it seemed logical that the company would take advantage of the fact that they could stop spending money on legal fees and drop the case altogether.

However, after a brief and frustrating phone call with my attorney, I learned that my former employer had no intention of changing course at all. They were content to have me sidelined and effectively unable to compete.

So even though Dempsey's fate was now running an eerie parallel to mine, nothing material was changing. My actions would still be restricted. The lawsuit would proceed.

I was sitting at my cubicle at the corporate office in Detroit when I saw my phone light up with Dempsey's name. I'd been reading an email and trying to figure out how to respond, and suddenly, with one glance at the name of the caller, the world had compressed itself so that the only two things that existed were me and the ringing phone.

It had been about eighteen months since I'd first been served those papers at my parents' house, eighteen months since I'd had any communication with Dempsey at all. I stared at the phone until the screen returned to black, my stomach already in knots, my heart pumping the same way it used to when he called, my face instantly flushed, my reaction to seeing his name apparently permanently programmed inside me.

Dempsey left a voicemail that I listened to immediately, and he asked me to call him back.

I wish I could say that this was the moment that I chose to simply let it all go, to really move on with my life, to make the decision to truly be done with Dempsey. So much had happened and everything, from school to work to attending conferences, was measurably harder with the lawsuit always pulsing in the background of my life. I wish I could say that I no longer felt that pull toward him that I always felt, that gravity, which was maybe loyalty or maybe guilt or maybe love, or some mixture of all of those things—but I can't say that, so I got up from my desk and walked outside and found a picnic table by the parking lot to sit on. It was a beautiful Midwestern day with a bright yellow sun tacked to the corner of a sky the color of a robin's egg, a slash of clouds adding texture to the blue, and I dialed his number and listened to it ring once. His voice was the same as it always was when he answered, quiet and low with a sense of seriousness, and I felt the same as I always did, nervous and excited and eager, and he said, "Tim, listen, I'm sorry I was such a dick," and I laughed and said, "Shit, it's all right, it's water under the bridge," and he laughed hard, and I did too, but the entire time I knew that it really wasn't all water under the bridge because I was still hamstrung by the lawsuit, and it felt like my job was falling apart, and I wasn't sure how much longer I would have it either—the cracks had begun to show—but I didn't want him to be mad at me anymore, I didn't want him to be disappointed, so I said it again, "Shit, man, it's all water under the bridge at this point."

The conversation went on like that for a few minutes, with him telling me what he was up to and talking about his lawsuit, and I listened the way I always did, trying to sound smart and witty and funny. When it was over, I sat there on the picnic table, unsure of what to call the feeling that I had in that moment. It was somewhere between glad to have talked with him and repulsed with myself for so quickly falling back into my usual role, practically salivating for his attention.

From my spot on the picnic table, I watched as a car backed out of its parking spot, its red brake lights glowing just before its white reverse lights flicked off. It drove slowly toward the exit. Seconds later, it was gone.

I stood up and turned toward the building that I worked in, toward the job that I knew wasn't working out, and wished, not for the first time, that I had a crystal ball to tell me how my future would play out. I'd known that I couldn't stay with Dempsey for even one more minute. What I hadn't known, though, was just how hard it was going to be to make it without him.

I settled the lawsuit two years after it had all started, but it had served its purpose. It had ruined my chances of success in my new role, and my employer had paid more than a hundred thousand dollars in legal fees, not to mention the tuition they'd paid for me to attend school. I'd brought in next to no business due to the TRO and the limitations on whom I could talk to, and it was clear to both of us that I was a losing investment that had cost them a considerable amount of money. Over the course of one conversation with my boss, and a subsequent follow-up email, we agreed to part ways amicably.

Now, more than a decade after the lawsuit settled, I can see that the price I paid for leaving Dempsey was exactly the right price. Which isn't to say that I deserved all of Dempsey's fury, but what I learned during those eight years I worked for him, and the two years I spent defending myself in that lawsuit, while my criminal background and failures as a father were brought up over and over as a way of questioning my character, when my past was laid out before me and presented as an indictment, was that the fundamental lesson I learned early in sobriety—to accept the things I cannot change and find the courage to change the things I can—was the lesson I would benefit from the most.

Years after all of that, though, after meeting my wife on a train ride downtown, after finishing both my undergraduate and graduate degrees, after starting my own business and using so many of the lessons I learned from Dempsey about grit and perseverance, about hard work, I sat with him at a small metal table outside a coffee shop in Annapolis, Maryland. Across the street the water glistened in the harbor. We hadn't seen each other in years, and we'd never spoken about the lawsuit and what had happened. I was nervous to be there, and maybe he was too, and then we began talking, his voice quiet in just the way I remembered, and he lit up a cigar, his eyes squinting as he cupped his hand around the wooden match, the smoke swirling around the table, the smell as familiar as family, as familiar as home, and it was good to be together, to see him, even with all that had happened.

I would never quite fully understand what had transpired between us, or even what to call it, and I would spend years trying to unpack what had happened in that time with him, remembering the pain of it all, the toxicity, but remembering the joy of it too, the excitement, the thrill, the love I felt—and still feel—for him. I would wonder, over and over, what debt I owed, or if, indeed, I owed him anything at all. In order to grow, to heal, I had to leave his anger behind, but that also meant leaving him behind, and I still haven't figured out what, if anything, that means.

I saw him from time to time over the years—at conferences we both attended. I was always nervous to see him, but also glad, and I'd catch up with him while he sat at an outdoor table, often under a palm tree, smoking his cigar, his eyes watching everything around him, missing nothing, a plan forever hatching in his mind. But I could never fully shake the role I fell right back into in his presence. He was always the boss, and this man who had saved my life, and I was forever the twenty-six-year-old trying to prove himself. I was a puppy sitting expectantly at his feet, looking for attention, and no matter how aware of it I was, or how much I tried to change the way I acted and felt, I literally couldn't.

A couple of years ago, my phone again lit up with his name, and I let it go to voicemail. The next day came an email, and then a text, and then another phone call.

When I answered, he immediately launched into a story about what he was doing now, and the company he was trying to build. I listened intently, all of it feeling so incredibly familiar, even the business idea itself, and the way he was explaining it. He needed my help, he said. "I'm getting the band back together."

I told him I was happy for him, and that it sounded interesting, and that I was sure he would be successful, but I also liked the way things were between us now and I didn't want to jeopardize the progress we'd made. "I'm so grateful for everything you did for me, and for everything you taught me, but I can't work for you again," I said, aware that I was still not courageous enough to say the word "won't." He said, "What do you mean?" and I said, "Well, that lawsuit really fucked me up for a long time," and he said, "What lawsuit?" and I stood there in my home office, the phone glued to my ear, confused, and then stunned, that he had no idea what I was talking about. It dawned on me in that exact moment that there are things in life that can be absolutely universe-shifting for one person, experiences that can change the entire trajectory of one's life, sequences of events put into motion by one individual that can be so fundamentally significant, so fundamentally impactful for one person, while being nothing more than a shoulder shrug for the other person.

It was also in that moment, after I had declined the invitation to work with him again, that the tone of the conversation shifted. His voice was now clipped, and building in intensity, and I could imagine his jaw clenched on the other end of the phone, just like it used to be. "You're going to let some fucking bullshit from the past affect this shit now?" he said in a way that I knew was rhetorical. "All that fucking shit I did for you, *all that fucking shit*, and you're not going to waltz with the guy who took you to the motherfucking dance?"

Regardless of how much time had passed, I'm not certain I ever really thought that he had changed, but it was now clear that he was the same as he had ever been. When I spoke, my words came out much more fluidly, and much more confidently, buoyed by the fact that getting a taste of the old him, that old fire-breathing dragon, made it so much easier to feel secure in my decision to leave, and to say what I said next. "Yeah, Sean, that's what I'm saying. I'm not going to work with you ever again."

He didn't respond. Instead, he just ended the call. I stood there in the silence, my heart racing, my adrenaline feeding my anger and frustration, ready to put my right hand through the center of my computer monitor, or tear a picture off the wall, but I instead took a deep breath and steadied myself, trying to take solace in what I knew was the right choice—to never work with him again.

EPILOGUE

It's possible that part of me did think he'd changed. Or part of me wanted to believe he had. I still had this fantasy where he found a way to deal with his anger, and I found a way to be a different person when I was around him, and we somehow chiseled out a relationship that was different from the one we'd had.

Even now, I still struggle to contextualize and name Dempsey's behavior toward me. It feels incredibly complicated. Was it abusive? Maybe. But even if it was, it was an abuse I felt I deserved, and an abuse I think I needed. I'm not sure I would have responded to anything different. And I wonder if, in that case, the end justifies the means.

I'll be forever grateful to Dempsey for what he did for me—plucking me out of a dead-end restaurant job and showing me the world of business, giving me the opportunity to get sober, supporting me as I established a relationship with my daughter. Simultaneously, I sometimes think that I never want to see him again. It's a complicated space to inhabit.

In just a few years I'll be fifty, the same age Dempsey was when he sold his company. From this vantage point, I can finally adopt at least some of his perspective. I can finally think about what his life was like when he first gave me that job, when he was building his company, when he was dealing with all the stress and pressure of growing a business. I can think now about how frustrated I must have made him, over and over, as he watched me struggle to grow up, to get sober, to become a responsible person.

I remember a time right before he sent me to rehab, when my drinking and using was at its worst. I'd become indebted to my roommate Richie—he'd often cover me at the bar, or pay for my portion of the bills, or buy groceries and household supplies—and we'd agreed that when I got paid next, I'd repay part of what I owed him. The problem—there was always a problem in those years— was that I got paid on Fridays, and we'd gone out the night before, drinking and snorting lines of cocaine until the birds began chirping. I'd called in sick to work that Friday, which meant I wouldn't be there to pick up my paycheck.

Richie had been looking forward to the money, and he was upset with me that I didn't have it—one of the few moments of tension we'd ever had—so on Saturday, when no one was at the office, Richie dropped me off in front of the building. I used my keycard to get past security then rode the elevator up to the thirty-fifth floor and entered the office. I knew the office manager, Janet, kept her office unlocked, and I knew where she hid the key to the filing cabinet that I was certain held my paycheck. So I went into her office and grabbed the key. I unlocked the cabinet, located the check, locked everything back up, and left.

When I got into the office at 8:30 Monday morning, Dempsey and Janet were waiting for me. Dempsey was furious, and not in the way that he usually was. Instead, he was furious in a way that was simultaneously incredibly angry and utterly disappointed. I tried to explain myself, but even back then, even in that state, I knew how out of line my behavior was.

Dempsey threatened to call the police, and Janet seemed truly hurt that I would betray her trust in that way—we'd established a close relationship, bonding over Dempsey's fury, which we both received in nearly equal amounts. I felt small and ashamed of myself, and I told them as much, knowing that my words must have sounded hollow. How could they not? In the end, they both forgave me. Not long afterward, Dempsey sent me to rehab.

I own a business now, and I think often about what it would be like to have an employee do to me what I did to Dempsey. Like Dempsey, I'd be furious and disappointed. Unlike Dempsey, I'm not sure I could move past it.

When I look at this story from Dempsey's point of view, it seems even more impossible to believe. Dempsey changed my existence in enormous and significant ways, in ways that gave me a chance at a life, at a real, beautiful, precious life unburdened by addiction, one that I've been able to nurture and expand and relish, one for which I have a deep and visceral gratitude.

But I'm not sure what, if anything, I gave Dempsey in return.

Which I know isn't the point. But it does illustrate how unbalanced and surprising life can be, how one person's random act of generosity can set into motion a sequence of events that ripples across decades, across generations. I'm twenty years sober now. I'm a father and a husband. None of it would have been possible without Dempsey.

The language to tell this story has been hard to come by. I've spent nearly a decade writing it, and I'm still not sure I've done it justice. I'm still not sure I've entirely captured what that man did for me, and what it means that he did it.

In so many ways, this story feels uniquely mine. But I know that it's also his. He would tell it differently, though. And rightly so. I'm not sure which parts he would remember, or which parts would matter to him. Or if any of it would matter at all.

What I've come to know in the years since all of this is that Dempsey—by giving me a job, by sending me to rehab, by being so incredibly hard on me—helped me begin to see myself, to see that I was so much more than I believed I was. Rehab, AA meetings, boxing, running, writing—I now see that they were all paths to self-assessment, by which I mean self-reflection, avenues I took to see myself more clearly, techniques I used to, as Carl Jung put it, make the unconscious conscious.

When I look out over the horizon of time that exists between then and now, at the implausibility of it all, of being a waiter in that one restaurant that one man happened to frequent, I'm overcome with gratitude—to Dempsey, yes, but also to all the people who saw something in me I simply couldn't see in myself. Without him, without them, my life would have been different in ways that are unimaginable to me.

It's difficult to know how to wrap up a story like this one, a story that hasn't really ended yet, a story that remains, in many ways, unresolved. So I have to settle for what these pages have given me, which is a way to remember exactly how I got from that Baker's Square restaurant to where I am now, which is smack-dab inside the nucleus of a beautiful, sober life that continues to unfold in the city of Chicago, the city I love so much, not far from the intersection of Wacker Drive and Monroe Street, where a glass and steel high-rise springs from the concrete, where I'm certain the thirty-fifth floor still smells faintly of cigars.

Acknowledgments

Writers make books, but people make writers, and there have been lots of them who have helped shape me into the writer I am today.

Thank you to Courtney Ochsner for seeing what this book could be, and for believing in it, and then acquiring it, and to the wonderful team at the University of Nebraska Press for turning the words I wrote into a book for the second time. I couldn't be more grateful.

Thank you to Michele Morano, for reading early versions of this book not once, but twice, and for saying what needed to be said not once, but twice, and for being the kind of mentor a writer dreams of having, one who's both kind and brilliant, and incredibly talented, and always setting a bar that's just out of reach. Thank you, too, for more than a decade of friendship. I count myself lucky to know you.

Thank you to Penny Guisinger for your magnificent insight about the end of the book, and for pushing me to rewrite it, and for helping me figure out exactly what it was I was trying to say.

Thank you to Amanda Kabak, for sharing the ups and downs of the writing life with me, and for finding endless, ceaseless, limitless rejection just as maddeningly funny (is that the right word?) as I do.

Thank you to Mike Chalmers for fifteen-plus incredible years of friendship, and business travails, and runs, and fights, and Burkholder's rolls (RIP), and conversations about books and writing and life. I can't wait to read your memoir.

Thank you to the writers I know and love, and whom I'm unquestionably fortunate to call my friends: Melanie Brooks, Alexis Paige, Hope Edelman, Barrie Jean Borich, Chris Green, Miles Harvey,

Tony St. Clair, and the late Ned Stuckey-French, whom I miss and think of often.

Thank you to Katie Rowland for always being so generous with your time and emails, and for your editorial insights, and for helping me push my work forward.

Thank you to Jared Yates Sexton for passing along such an incredible opportunity to me back in 2019, and for writing a hell of a book on masculinity.

Thank you to my parents, Tom and Lor Visser, for all your support over the years, and to the rest of my family for continuing to show up for me—Heidi and Jon, Aaron and Lauren, Jillian and Ryan.

Thank you to all the people I met in the rooms of AA over the years. It was your stories and your courage that helped me stay sober.

Thank you to the staff at Hazelden Betty Ford, circa early 2005, for doing whatever it is you did during those fateful twenty-eight days.

Thank you to my beautiful and sensationally talented daughter, Haley Jade, for letting me back in your life all those years ago, and for becoming such a kind, generous, hardworking, and creative young woman. You may not see it yet, but you will soon: The world is yours for the taking.

And finally, to my true ride or die, my stunningly patient, gracious, and gorgeous wife, Erin, whose endless support allows me to do what I do, and whose partnership has given me a life beyond my wildest imagination. I love you now, and always.

To order or obtain more information on these or other University of Nebraska Press titles, visit nebraskapress.unl.edu.